*Change the Lapel Pin*

*Personalizing Leadership to Transform Organizations and Communities*

**By Alex Johnson, PhD**

Published by:
Smart Business Network
835 Sharon Drive, Suite 200
Westlake, OH  44145

Printed in the United States of America
Contributor: Dennis Seeds
Editor: Dustin S. Klein

ISBN:  978-1-945389-70-2
Library of Congress Control Number:  2018943076

*I dedicate this book in loving memory to these beautiful women who helped me when I could not help myself, prayed for me before themselves, and taught me to believe:*

Marian Perry
Marion Johnson
Sarah Watts
Barbara Pharr
Marie Davis
Betty Davis
Ruby King
Callie Coaxum
Angela McCray
Nancy Agurs
Marianne Winick
Betty Morgan
Margie Edwards
Leola Bell
Daphne Johnson

# Change the Lapel Pin: Personalizing Leadership for Organizations and Communities

Foreword

   I. Introduction   ...................................................................I
  II. The Remnants and Rudiments of My Personalized Approach ...............1
     Coming of Age .......................................................................4
     My Leadership Journey ........................................................19
  III. Connecting the Fundamentals of the Personalized Approach .............33
  IV. Charting the Three Essentials of Leadership .........................................39
   V. Understanding and Applying the Origins of Leadership .....................49
  VI. Competencies and Skills for Starting and
     Growing as a Leader ..........................................................63
     Advice for Incoming Leaders ........................................................66
     Engaging the Organization ..........................................................83
     Culture as a Context for Organizational Transformation ...........97
  VII. Other Considerations in Refining
     Your Personalized Approach .....................................................111
     Leader as Manager to Attain Organizational Excellence
       Through the Uninterrupted Cycle of Leadership Effectiveness (UnCLE) ........114
     Images of Leadership: How Does it Look and Feel .....................128
     Acknowledging Perils and Pitfalls ..............................................142
     Diversity as a Condition for Success in a Global Economy ........154
     The Future of Leadership ........................................................174
  VIII. Lagniappe ...........................................................................187

Acknowledgements ..............................................................................195
Notes ..............................................................................198

# Foreword

In an era when continuous improvement is the norm, leaders at all levels must be adept at managing the constant and unrelenting change required to make their organizations more responsive and successful.

Community college leaders share this responsibility. As president and CEO of the American Association of Community Colleges, or AACC, which represents the interests of more than 1,100 two-year institutions and 12.2 million students nationwide, I know firsthand the pressures placed on the shoulders of leaders as they seek to advance their institutions.

Among the many demands they face is the growing need to produce more highly skilled workers, the requirement to graduate students in greater numbers and more quickly, the effects of eroding public funding, and the urgency to increase access and educational attainment of minority students.

In carrying-out the AACC mission of building a nation of learners by advancing America's community colleges, I believe that our role is to provide emerging and existing leaders with the skills needed for institutional transformation. Through this preparation, leaders will be better equipped to develop a dependable and reliable system that allows them to transfer what they learn into successful practice now and into the future.

This is the type of transition that is accommodated through *Change the Lapel Pin: Personalizing Leadership for Organizations and Communities*. Dr. Johnson does an outstanding job of introducing a philosophy of leadership that comes from within, personalized from a blend of education, experience, and exposure. Included, too, are applicable competencies and skills learned before and during the job. Applying natural talent when leading and the ability to address change through innovative practices round out the approach.

The organic nature of the Change the Lapel model also reminds me of the importance of authentic leadership, in which technical competence and interpersonal skill mesh to advance both the organization and the individual. Dr. Johnson provides poignant examples of this integration through his experiences and those of other leaders like Jeff Bezos of Amazon and Howard Schultz of Starbucks. In this regard, and in consideration of the works by Lee Bolman and Terrence Deal, especially *Leading with Soul*, the Change the Lapel Pin model not only emphasizes the hands and the heads of leaders, but also the deeper and more enduring elements of courage, spirit, and hope.

Dr. Johnson has demonstrated the success of the Change the Lapel Pin model in his various presidencies. I had the privilege of working very closely with him in Louisiana, where he led the transformation of Delgado Community College as the institution and community recovered from Hurricane Katrina. Moreover, in leading the Community College of Allegheny County and now Cuyahoga Community College, he has built upon the stature of two great institutions by establishing programs of innovation and excellence using the Change the Lapel Pin model.

While Dr. Johnson's achievements in higher education are the backdrop for *Change the Lapel Pin: Personalizing Leadership for Organizations and Communities*, based on my experience in leadership development, I am confident that the book will benefit leaders universally. Thus, in my opinion, it is a must-read volume for any emerging or existing leader who wishes to create a unique approach to leadership.

Walter G. Bumphus, PhD
President and CEO
American Association of Community Colleges

# I. Introduction

*"Thus out of small beginnings greater things have been produced..."*
— *William Bradford*

The answer to the question, "Does leadership really matter?" is yes. And there are numerous examples of why this is true. As an illustration, I have observed instances in the past where leaders of large companies (like Yahoo, United Airlines, EquiFax, and Mylan, to name a few) were directly responsible for public debacles.

If this trend continues, and I expect it might, we are headed for a leadership crisis in our country that threatens the extent to which governments, businesses, and organizations can effectively serve the American people. This predicament, which has the potential to erode public trust, is evident now in troubling examples of leaders at every level who are self-absorbed and lack understanding of the fundamental principles and skills needed to transform systems and organizations.

The 2016 presidential race was an example of such an environment, as both candidates focused on self-promotion and vitriol, rather than conveying how their policies and practices as the Commander-in-Chief would help Americans provide for themselves and generations to come. In his victory speech, the eventual winner, Donald John Trump, vowed to unite the nation, a difficult proposition indeed, given the divisiveness his campaign engendered during the primary and general elections. To date, it appears he has some work ahead to accomplish his goal of bringing the nation together.

In the private sector, the vestiges of the country's 2008 financial crisis remain as businesses continued unscrupulous practices. Among the companies with more publicized incidents is Wells Fargo and Company, whose employees began in 2011 to secretly create millions of unauthorized bank and credit card accounts—without customers knowing it. The phony accounts earned the bank unwarranted fees and allowed employees to boost sales figures and earn bonuses. After the abuses came to light, the bank fired 5,300 employees and, ultimately, Chairman and CEO John Stumpf was forced to resign.

Leadership problems are not restricted to business and government. College leaders are also not without fault. The nation's faith and trust were shaken in the 1970s and 1980s amid charges that higher education could not demonstrate accountability for their missions. Some athletes, for example, were graduating from institutions and unable to read. One of the most well-known cases involved Kevin Ross, who graduated from high school in 1979 with only the ability to read his name and school on his diploma. He was accepted into Creighton University to play basketball. After three injury-prone seasons, he dropped out at the age of 23 and returned to elementary school, where he was taught to read by the famous educator, Marva Collins.

Unfortunately, issues associated with higher education continue. Recently, several institutions' academic reputations were irretrievably scarred because of issues surrounding, once again, their athletic programs. Notable among these cases is the University of North Carolina at Chapel Hill. Often referred to as a "public Ivy," the university barely escaped stiff penalties by the National Collegiate Athletic Association (NCAA) amid allegations it offered poor quality coursework with few requirements, ostensibly, to keep athletes eligible. The NCAA concluded, after a very long and arduous investigation, that there were no violations of its rules. That is was an academic infraction, not an athletic one. Thus, the university was placed on probation and ongoing monitoring by its accrediting body, the Southern Association for Colleges and Schools (SACS). The SACS enforces academic and institutional standards that, when violated, can result in the suspension of degrees, programs, and services, including federally-based financial aid.

When you consider leaders' shortcomings, generally ineffective leadership affects employee satisfaction and well-being. In a publication entitled "Poor Leadership," researchers E. Kevin Kelloway, Niro Sivanathan, Lori Francis, and Julian Barling offered evidence of how poor leadership contributes to employee discomfort caused by faulty interpersonal relations, lack of supervisor support, and career concerns. Issues with job scheduling and workload were also linked to management incompetence by the authors.

Fortunately, there are examples of passionate, progressive, and authentic individuals in the private and public sectors that can, although less publicized, serve as examples of effective leadership.

Thomas Mann, senior fellow at the Brookings Institution, and Norman Ornstein, resident scholar at the American Enterprise Institute, share that optimism. They suggest such illustrations present the opportunity to create a legacy of future leaders who will address today's challenges.

From these examples—and the application of proven principles and characteristics of leadership—it is therefore possible to create a new paradigm of how to systematically develop, nourish, and apply personalized leadership. This premise underlies, in part, the purpose for *Change the Lapel Pin: Personalizing Leadership to Transform Organizations and Communities*, which is to present current and prospective leaders with a way to personalize leadership and eliminate faulty, unreliable practices by combining formal training, work and life experience, and the characteristics of successful leaders—and people.

This combination of influences and factors comprises

what I call the Three Essentials of Leadership: education, experience, and exposure. They represent the core of the personalized leadership system and must be assessed to identify instances that are critical as you develop your leadership approach.

Setting the stage for this process is chapter two, where I provide a retrospective on the foundations of my approach, which may have impetus as you begin developing yours.

In chapter three, I provide a graphic illustration of the fundamentals of the approach, which are described more fully in subsequent chapters of the book.

In chapter four, the Three Essentials are defined and discussed in the context of my personal references in the areas of education, experience, and exposure.

In chapter five, I discuss natural traits that accentuate the Three Essentials. These traits are primarily motivation, temperament, dominance, and aptitude—which, once identified and developed, can provide more substance to your personalized approach. In some instances, natural tendencies can also serve as a deterrent to your success. Being ill-tempered, risk-adverse, or impersonal are behaviors that must be avoided in the workplace and replaced with more productive forms of behavior that include emotional intelligence and other qualities.

Another key ingredient in support of the Three Essentials (and critical to personalizing your leadership approach) are skills and competencies for success in your initial leadership role and throughout your career. In chapter six of *Change the Lapel Pin*, I offer an overview of these specific organizational and management techniques.

No leadership approach, including the personalized one based on the Three Essentials, is complete without learned behaviors that add depth to your work. These are discussed in chapter seven. They often materialize over the course of your career, but can be more valuable early on. The capacity to look and act like a leader, manage as a leader, recognize and eliminate challenges, and provide for your ongoing development and that of your colleagues can add a dimension to your approach that many leaders do not immediately possess.

And in chapter eight, Lagniappe, I provide essentially closing remarks on why I believe that, while not a magic elixir, the personalized approach can bolster reliability and consistency in leadership when organizations and communities need it the most.

The term "change the lapel pin" emerged from an experience during the start of my presidency at Delgado Community College in New Orleans, Louisiana. I replaced an existing lapel pin with another version depicting the seal of the college. The change, albeit small, resulted in inquiries about why the action was warranted. From the experience I deduced several things. First, I learned that physical manifestations of leadership are powerful. Next, the response enabled me to unveil my hopes and aspirations for the institutions. And, finally, it allowed me to think more carefully about my approach to leadership.

From this, and other experiences, *Change the Lapel Pin: Personalizing Leadership to Transform Organizations and Communities* was conceived.

The book presents a fundamental system where I call upon prospective and existing heads of organizations to weave together their most valuable assets—education, experience, and exposure—to create a personalized and integrated approach to leadership. By recognizing and strengthening these areas, and refining them through applications in the workplace, continuous professional development, and strategies in response to internal and external factors, the chances for success increase.

In the end, you will discover this book is not a conventional treatment of leadership presented by individuals who have had little or no leadership development or experience. Nor is it a professional development program with "cafeteria-style" courses and activities that offer little or no value in the workplace. Instead, it introduces a paradigm shift in how you develop and act as a leader. The term "change the lapel pin" is symbolic of this shift, both in theory and action, as new and veteran leaders operate and advance contemporary systems and organizations.

*Alex Johnson, PhD*
*Cleveland, Ohio*
*June, 2018*

# II. The Remnants and Rudiments of My Personalized Approach

*"The pivotal moments in your life are always*
*made up of smaller pieces,*
*things that seemed insignificant at the time,*
*but in fact, brought you to*
*where you needed to be."*

— *Elizabeth Norris*

Leadership is not an absolute. There are no universal principles that allow only good days in the role. If this is the type of experience you desire, then neither leadership nor this book are meant for you. Leading is as rewarding and vexing as real life. In real life, we learn from our experiences and mistakes, hoping that when we encounter the same or a similar incident somewhere down the road, we are better equipped to handle it. Likewise, experienced leaders, through trial and error and occasional dumb luck, fashion a reliable approach from pieces of life and work. This evolution, however, takes time. And some leaders find themselves struggling because they are not equipped to either run an organization or respond to the challenges within it.

> *Leadership is not an absolute. There are no universal principles that allow only good days in the role.*

*Change the Lapel Pin* is meant to help you develop as a leader. And as you do so, it is necessary to look back and identify situations that shaped your personal convictions and ideals. These experiences—both positive and negative—are evident in many leaders, but some underestimate the experiences' impact on their leadership principles and behaviors and, thus, do not embrace them. In the following sections of this chapter, I give anecdotal examples of how my foundations launched my leadership journey and gave impetus to my approach encompassed in the Three Essentials—education, experience, and exposure. I encourage you to compare your own current qualities and foundations to those I present. Much of this material is based on my 40 years of personal experience in higher education as a faculty member and administrator, 25 of which have been as a president. During my journey, I have experienced and learned something about leadership that can be applied in the college setting and beyond. Accordingly, I am confident the Three Essentials as presented here are a foundation for launching and advancing your career in the increasingly complex world of leadership.

To get a glimpse of this world, you need look no further than higher education. Increased pressures on presidents—particularly in the public sector—including state politics, budget troubles, and misalignment with trustees and athletics are undermining the focus on academics.

This environment affects the average tenure that presidents remain in their roles. When I began in higher education in 1978, it was not unusual for college chiefs to stay in their posts for one or more decades. Since 2006, however, the average tenure for college presidents has decreased from 8.5 years to 5.6 years. Further, two decades ago just 13 percent of presidents were over the age of 60. Today, that percentage is 58.

These statistics demonstrate just how challenging college presidencies have become and, by extension, are an example of the general worries of leadership introduced earlier. This environment can be deleterious to both present and aspiring leaders unless they are equipped with a system of leadership built around their individual experiences, attainments and talents, combined with specific competencies. As you read this book, hopefully you will be able to conduct your own personal assessment.

# Coming of Age

In the Brazilian Amazon, young boys belonging to the indigenous Sateré-Mawé tribe mark their coming of age when they turn 13 through the bullet ant tradition. They search the jungle for bullet ants, which are sedated and submerged in an herbal solution. The ants are then woven into gloves with the stingers pointed inwards. An hour or so later, the ants wake up angry and the initiation begins. Each boy must wear the gloves for 10 minutes. Enduring the pain demonstrates the boys' readiness for manhood, so few cry out, as doing so would demonstrate weakness. Each boy will eventually wear the gloves 20 times over the span of several months before the initiation is complete.

Most of us can recall specific events or a period, maybe not as traumatic or excruciating as the Sateré-Mawé, which marked the symbolic or actual transition from one stage of life to the next, culminating in who we have become. Occasionally, this transition takes many years to occur, as was my case.

As I look back over my life, the experiences I encountered during the 1950s, '60s, and '70s added impetus to my leadership approach. Represented in this brief period of the nation's 240–plus year existence were the largest gains in social equality in its history. For me, these 30 years had a profound effect personally and professionally. They shaped, in part, the leadership strategies espoused in this book.

Unfortunately, the three decades from 1950 to 1980 were preceded by almost a century of structural segregation that began just after the 1865 enactment of the Thirteenth Amendment of the U.S. Constitution. That amendment eliminated legal slavery but also sparked a string of segregationist laws and measures in southern states which essentially acted to keep those emancipated mired in institutionalized servitude.

Just before the start of the 1900s, several campaigns emerged which objected to the harsh realities that African Americans faced in their daily lives: the Niagara Movement, which led to the creation of the National Association for the Advancement of Colored People (NAACP); the Universal Negro Improvement Association; and the National Negro Business League. These three groups were among the early organizations that provided the foundation for a more expansive effort to oppose disenfranchisement based on race.

These efforts were followed by the 1954 landmark U.S. Supreme Court decision, Brown v. Board of Education, which arguably launched the modern day Civil Rights Movement. In it, the Supreme Court ruled that segregation in public schools throughout the country was unconstitutional, and ordered states to move with "deliberate speed" to implement its findings.

Despite this directive, the decision did not immediately change my life. My experience in Concord, North Carolina (a little segregated town where I was raised located just 17 miles east of Charlotte) was not transformed. I continued to enroll in schools and worship at a church that were built for black folk only. I attended a segregated movie theater, where blacks sat in the balcony. And my family still shopped at a department store where we were not permitted to try on the clothes before purchasing them.

It was not until 1960 when my parents decided to relocate our family to New York City in pursuit of better jobs and a freer existence that I experienced life in an integrated society, with one exception. Where I lived in eastern Harlem there were only people who looked like me.

Our family move was in concert with the Second Great Migration, which lasted from 1941 to 1970. It was a period where many African-Americans moved to take jobs in the burgeoning industrial cities throughout America.

The simple freedoms of eating and shopping where you desired, sharing public accommodations with white folk, and visiting the rich cultural centers of the city on days other than those assigned to your race, were liberating. Harlem in some respects was a cultural and political center. It was distinguished for its commitment to celebrating black heritage and exploring the benefits of black activism versus civil disobedience.

Despite this socially progressive environment, underneath its surface Harlem was essentially an enclave where the economic benefit was accorded exclusively to outsiders—store owners and landlords—who did not live in the community nor employ its residents. Social services and public safety were also administered by individuals who did not reside in Harlem. And it was this oppressive environment, along with the momentum around political activism, that eventually fueled the 1964 riots that erupted when a teen was shot by a police officer.

James Powell was attending summer school at Robert Wagner Junior High School located in Yorkville, which at the time was a predominately working-class white area on the Upper East Side of Manhattan. He became involved in an altercation with Patrick Lynch, the superintendent of three apartment houses, after Lynch hosed some black students who had congregated on the stoops of one of his buildings.

During the incident, Powell chased Lynch into one the buildings. When Powell exited, an off-duty police lieutenant, Thomas Gilligan, who witnessed the scene from a nearby shop, ran to the scene and shot the 15-year-old Powell. His death sparked six days of rioting that began in central Harlem and spread to the predominantly black Bedford-Stuyvesant section of Brooklyn.

I was going on 14 years old at the time of Powell's death. The incident marked the first time I heard about a child being killed by a police officer. It shed my innocence of youth and made me vulnerable at a very early age. Because of this, Harlem, to me, was no longer the cultural and social icon I had previously experienced.

I was not the only one who had a visceral response to the upheaval in Harlem that summer. It became a major concern for President Lyndon Johnson, no less. Following Powell's death and the riots, the next summer Johnson established Project Uplift as a component of his Great Society. Project Uplift was intended to prevent the recurrence of the riots by employing thousands of youth in a variety of jobs to keep them busy and off the streets. I was one of those people who found employment that summer of 1965.

During the summer of 1966, leading to my senior year in high school, I visited Concord, the home of my maternal grandparents, Marion and Willie Johnson. By this time, segregation was outlawed by the Civil Rights Act of 1964, which banned discrimination based on race, color, religion, sex, or national origin. It ended unequal application of voter registration requirements and racial segregation in schools, at the workplace, and in any facilities that served the general public.

The act was the culmination of many people's selflessness: those who participated in the bus boycott in Montgomery, Alabama, that led to the eventual desegregation of public transportation in that town; the youth who led the desegregation of Little Rock, Arkansas' Central High School, among the first staunchly segregationist schools in the south to comply with Brown v. Board of Education; and the "freedom riders," comprised mostly of college students, black and white alike, who were instrumental in improving voter rights in Mississippi.

During my visit to Concord, I appreciated the new freedom and slower pace of activity in comparison to New York. Most of my childhood friends were driving; something I could never do as a 16-year-old in New York. To get my driver's license, I urged my grandmother—under the pretense of helping her with household chores—to let me finish my final year of high school in Concord. She agreed with one stipulation, that I attend the previously all-white Concord High School instead of the still all-black Logan High School. And so, I became one of four black students attending Concord High School that 1966-67 school year.

I believed the teachers and administrators wanted this new arrangement to work, but I never could quite overcome the sense that I—and the other black students—was assigned to a special category of people they had no experience educating, but who they had to accept because of the legal requirement.

Though I never experienced blatant disrespect, there were perhaps some teachers and students who believed I did not belong there. There were also those, however, who seemed genuinely interested in my well-being.

### Chester Misenheimer, guider of students
Among those in the latter group was our class guidance counselor Chester Misenheimer, who I met with twice during that initial school year. The first time was to develop my class schedule and the next after I received my score of

750 on the SAT. Misenheimer did not want me to concede a college education because my test results were not good enough for the University of North Carolina or Duke.

To be honest, I wasn't even considering attending college. Misenheimer recommended, however, that I explore the state's historically black colleges (HBCUs). With this encouragement, I applied to three of them. All accepted me. But, I chose to attend Winston-Salem State University (WSSU) a choice for which I have been truly thankful. Misenheimer was confident that my average grades and subpar SAT score could get me enrolled in a HBCU. I do not imagine, however, that he envisioned it would be the experience of a lifetime which served as the foundation for both my views on the importance of education to advance individuals and communities and my perspectives on leadership.

### The promise of black colleges

Colleges exclusively for black citizens were started during Jim Crow, or the "separate but equal" era, mainly by white benefactors like Henry Lyman Morehouse—an abolitionist and leader of the American Baptist Home Mission Society. Named in his honor is Morehouse College, the *alma mater* of Dr. Martin Luther King Jr. and many other significant leaders of African American descent.

WSSU, where I studied, began as Slater Industrial Academy and Normal School, whose responsibility, beginning in 1892, was to train individuals for teaching fields. I attended the university from 1967 to 1971, during a time that coincided with great social upheaval and activism in America. The struggle for equality expanded and involved other social issues such as free speech, women's rights, and the war in Vietnam. The equal rights era played out on the WSSU campus, heightened by the assassination on April 4, 1968, of Dr. Martin Luther King, Jr. In response to the devastating news, students gathered around the hallowed ground—called a "plot"—of Dr. King's fraternity, Alpha Phi Alpha. We paid homage to his legacy through words and familiar songs, like "We Shall Overcome."

Our sorrow escalated into outrage, which provoked us to march toward downtown Winston-Salem, North Carolina. At some point during the demonstration, police officers descended upon us, with rifles in tow, from squad cars with flashing blue lights. This action effectively halted our protest.

Although short-lived, our act served to celebrate Dr. King's life and legacy. We also reminded the nation that it had not completely ensured the basic right promised all Americans when it declared independence from Great Britain—that "all men are created equal, that they are endowed by their Creator with certain unalienable Rights, that among these are life, liberty, and the pursuit of happiness."

The Dr. King assassination also awakened the social consciousness of many WSSU students, leading them to pursue lives of uncompromising commitment to excellence and equality among the children they teach and within the communities they serve. My response was similar to my classmates, and undergirds other perspectives I stand for in carrying out my professional and civic roles.

In 1971, following graduation from WSSU, I returned to New York City and became a teacher in early childhood centers in the South Bronx. Working with young children in this urban setting only reinforced those ideals rooted in my commitment to equity in education. My subsequent graduate studies at Lehman College and Penn State provided the learning and relationships that gave them depth and breadth.

## Jack Traugott, spiritual advisor to the community

Another place beyond my colleges and universities provided a spiritual dimension to my focus on equality: St. John's Lutheran Church, where my mother, baby sister, Angela, and I found comfort in the words and works of its minister, Reverend Jack Traugott. He married Daphne and me and baptized our first child, Nakia.

Traugott, a white pastor of a nearly all-black congregation, exemplified the church's role in empowering family and individual growth through spiritual enlightenment, educational attainment, and civic engagement. His sermons on these subjects resonate with me still as I combine spiritual constructs with the technical competencies needed for leadership espoused in the Three Essentials.

Traugott's commitment can be likened to the admonishments of noted pastor and professor of theology, Barbara Brown Taylor. In her book, *Leaving Church: A Memoir of Faith*, she posits "What if churches blessed people for what they are doing in the world instead of chastening them for not doing more at church? What if church felt more like a way station than a destination? What if the church's job were to move people out the door, instead of trying to keep them in by convincing them that God needed them more in the world than in the church?" As a teacher of young children from the largely minority South Bronx, New York, with whose families I interacted with regularly, Traugott and Taylor's focus on community engagement greatly influenced me.

**The promise and power of the PhD**

Soon after marrying Daphne, while working at Tremont-Monterey Day Care Center in the Bronx, two of my college fraternity brothers, Chester Batts and Toney Grant, came for a visit. Batts and Grant were enrolled in doctoral programs at the University of Missouri. They talked about their experiences as though they were members of an exclusive club whose futures were assured. And, while they were bright, I quickly surmised if they could qualify for a prestigious graduate program, so could I.

For Batts and Grant, the PhD was all about just possessing it. But the essence of the doctorate was exemplified by Marianne Winick, my professor at Lehman College, where I completed a master's degree in 1973. Winick modeled how being a college professor could heighten your contribution to society through teaching, scholarship, and service—to the college and the community. Through her excellence in teaching and regular visits to the early childhood center, she inspired me to pursue a PhD, which would enable me to become a college professor like her. When she died in 2006, the college established an award in her memory. I was honored to be chosen as its first recipient.

In the mid-1970s, the Graduate Record Examination (GRE), one of the devices for assessing your worthiness for graduate work, offered minority examinees a chance to have their scores sent to colleges interested in enrolling students from diverse backgrounds. This GRE program, the Minority Student Locator Service, resulted in my receiving inquiries from several institutions—including the University of Pennsylvania, University of Pittsburgh, and Pennsylvania State University. Only Penn State, however, allowed me to select the major of my liking, early childhood education.

So, in the fall of 1975, Daphne, our little son, Nakia, and I moved to State College, Pennsylvania the home of Penn State. Our sendoff was reminiscent of the famous scene from the Frank Capra movie *It's a Wonderful Life*, which depicted the Martini Family moving from their dilapidated dwelling (owned by antagonist Henry F. Potter) to their new home in Bailey Park.

Like the Martini Family, we were encircled by friends and family who packed our tiny U-Haul for our journey of a lifetime to Penn State.

### Carol Cartwright, courageous advocate

Many things are memorable about my academic experience from 1975 to 1978 at Penn State, and most involve Carol Cartwright, my doctoral advisor and now dear friend.

First, Cartwright helped me understand that an important obligation is to develop relationships with the faculty that help you attain your ultimate goal. She assisted with this responsibility by surrounding me with her colleagues, who served on my dissertation committee, provided graduate assistantships that offset tuition and personal expenses, and invited me into their homes for social events.

At that time, an important requirement in doctoral programs was the comprehensive examinations, where you respond to questions in writing—and later orally—from your major professors on the cumulative content of your coursework. Just before I was scheduled for my written exams, Cartwright had to travel to Pittsburgh to be with her father, who had become very ill. She would not be present during my full day of written examinations. Her secretary, Anna Gajar, shared this news, adding that Cartwright was sorry about her absence and wished me luck. This was the kind of caring person she was.

An important final step in doctoral studies is development of the dissertation proposal. Essentially, you must prepare the first three chapters of your thesis that present an area to be studied, a review of the literature that substantiates this exploration, and a description of how you plan to carry out the study. By this time in my doctoral studies, I figured I was a fair writer. That is, until Cartwright reviewed my dissertation proposal. Her critique was so exhaustive that it made me question my capacity to complete the dissertation requirement. But it inspired me to become a better writer. I sent my doctoral committee the revised proposal, and during my oral defense it received high marks from all committee members except one, who took umbrage with the research design and later resigned from the committee.

I completed the PhD. It was a major accomplishment! Marianne Winick was the inspiration for it, and Carol Cartwright provided the substance. Cartwright was the most stabilizing force for my family and me throughout my doctoral studies. She provided numerous examples of professionalism and leadership, which I value and apply today. The team of faculty and staff she surrounded me with connoted the importance of a competent and committed team in identifying a sense of urgency and developing the strategies and tactics to address it.

The writing skills I developed because of Cartwright's critique of my dissertation proposal served me steadfastly as a faculty member and has helped me ascend to several administrative posts and experience success in those roles. As an aside, those writing skills remain superior to my speaking skills, which I am still perfecting.

Her expression of support during my comprehensive examinations, while responding to an ailing parent, modeled the importance of emotional intelligence in leadership. And since Penn State, she has presented many examples of the skills and dispositions required for success as a college president—a role in which she served proudly at Kent State University and Bowling Green State University.

I secured my first faculty position in 1978 at Bowling Green State University, teaching courses in both early childhood and special education. My colleagues were collegial, but competitive. The university rewarded exceptional teaching and scholarship, including publications and research. Excellence in these areas led to promotions, tenure, graduate faculty status and the financial security that comes with these designations. I was confident in this environment because of Carol's influence on me.

My experience at the university was overshadowed, however, by the harsh feelings about the institution held by some City of Bowling Green residents. Charges of elitism were often leveled by them, creating the sense that students—and in some instances, employees—of the university were not welcome. Several incidents were perceived to have racial overtones, and these led to the university creating a task force comprised of city and university representatives. I was invited to join the task force. In these sessions, I learned that an independent group cannot create a diverse and inclusive community when such a task is the responsibility of everyone in that community. That was an important lesson.

Eventually, Daphne and I agreed that while the university was a welcoming environment, the city was not where we wanted to raise our children. And so, when the opportunity came in 1981 to rejoin WSSU as a faculty member, I decided to move on.

In summary, the three decades—from my birth in 1950 through 1980—occurred during a time of significant social and cultural change in America. The modern Civil Rights Movement was unveiled and evolved to a point where other groups, formerly feeling alienated and disenfranchised, modeled it to ensure their rightful place in this country.

What happened during those three decades helped shape my views of the world and the perspectives that I have developed.

They gave root to my desire to foster inclusion, fairness, and the opportunity for education for each student attending the institutions for which I have been responsible.

They gave substance to my current belief in making opportunities for leadership open to everyone. These opportunities shape and enrich an individual's life and the future of an organization.

They also helped me understand I must be about the business of preparing successful citizens who, in the sentiments of Cornel West, situate themselves in the larger contexts of our community, who imagine a future rooted in the past, but who are keenly aware of the problems that will perplex us.

It is not unusual for life experiences to affect our career choices or leadership approaches. George Ambler in *How Experiences Shape and Make Leaders*, writes that experiences and our response to them are of critical importance in how leaders are formed and in what kind of leaders we become.

Ambler alludes to those instances you recall in your life which provided substance, direction and, ultimately, career choice. As you grow professionally, these experiences continue to have a profound effect by providing a framework for a stalwart, consistent, and principled approach to leadership and as a foundation for widening your growth and development. Every leader has a journey that shapes who they are.

### Rubie McCullough, advocate for families and children

Ambler's synopsis represents the case of Rubie McCullough, a renowned civic leader. She is one example of how life and professional experiences can contribute to becoming an effective leader in an organization and within the community.

McCullough was stalwart in her belief that residents of Cleveland, Ohio, should live in safe and well-appointed neighborhoods filled with amenities to aid the development of families and their children. In 1968, this was her main goal for establishing the Harvard Community Services Center. She presided over the organization for the next 21 years.

This was a goal deeply rooted in her childhood days in Enfield, North Carolina; dreamed up in the segregated schools she attended in that sweltering southern hamlet, and enriched during her days as a student at historically black North Carolina Central University.

When McCullough arrived in Cleveland in 1945, it was during the Second Great Migration. Many African Americans relocated from the South, seeking jobs and a better life. She came to Cleveland for a job, not in a factory, which was the norm, but with the Phyllis Wheatley Association, an organization that shared the same value systems that she developed growing up in Enfield. The Association was established in 1911 by McCullough's future mentor, Jane Edna Harris, with the goal of housing and helping unmarried African-American women and girls—

newcomers to the North often preyed upon by unscrupulous employers or agencies.

If growing up in segregated Enfield, North Carolina, fueled McCullough's passion and desire to improve the human condition, then the Phyllis Wheatley Association provided the experience for addressing it.

Soon after marrying, McCullough and her new husband moved to the eastern Cleveland neighborhood of Lee-Harvard, which stood in stark contrast to some inner-city communities where people settled; communities characterized by poor schools, inadequate policing, and deplorable housing. But even in Lee-Harvard, McCullough recognized that community and family development was necessary to keep it vibrant and attractive. It was then that she organized and founded the Harvard Community Services Center.

It was, indeed, the culmination of experiences in her segregated home state of North Carolina, her inspiring and rewarding work at the Phyllis Wheatley Association, and her tireless commitment to those in need that led to her leadership approach.

# My Leadership Journey

As you may have discerned, I have relied on the experiences of my youth and early adulthood to partially guide me through my nearly 40 years in higher education—including time as a faculty member, administrator, and the collective 25 years I have spent as a college president. It has not been a straight line of experiences that you might see on a resume. Instead, it has been a mixture of transactions and interactions with jobs and individuals. And it is the latter, people, that have had the most influence on my conduct as a leader. My successes often depended upon the extent I regarded them, and their willingness to follow me.

So, throughout my career, like Leonard Schaeffer, founding Chairman and CEO of WellPoint Networks, I have come to understand leadership is more than directives from the top. It is a partnership. As a long-standing college president, I have had to depend on my colleagues, the community, and so forth to ensure my leadership actions on behalf of students and the institution were successful. I have grown as a result. In this vein, and as Schaeffer notes, "leadership is not a state, it's a journey."

For me, this progression began in 1981 upon my return to Winston-Salem State University (WSSU) as a faculty member. I was committed to ensuring my teaching and scholarship added value to students in my courses. Recognition by "the administration" of my commitment resulted in appointments to committees charged with enriching the college experience for students. Surprisingly, during these activities, I developed an appreciation and broader understanding of the organization beyond the classroom.

I wanted to learn and do more. So, when I was asked by the university chancellor (equivalent of president) to consider an interim administrative post, I was humbled by the recognition and agreed. Returning to a "standard" work day was, perhaps, the most difficult aspect of the transition from teaching to administration, but the additional salary was an added incentive, as was the excitement I experienced over the prospect of helping more students benefit from college.

This assignment became permanent and was followed at that institution by two other administrative posts as the chancellor's executive assistant and, later, as a vice chancellor. Both positions provided immense supervisory responsibilities and allowed for a more thorough understanding of executive level duties and organization-wide initiatives, such as financial management, accreditation self-studies, and strategic planning.

My first presidency, in 1992 at Cuyahoga Community College, came about because of a telephone call from my friend, Carol Cartwright, who, at the time, was president of Kent State University. I was working at WSSU and surprised when Cartwright recommended a campus presidency at a two-year college.

I was at a university, so why would I consider a community college?

It is true I had developed a healthy respect and admiration for two-year institutions, but I never considered becoming the president of one.

The institution in question was based in Cleveland, Ohio, and led by her friend, Dr. Jerry Sue Thornton. Thornton came to Cuyahoga in September 1992, as its college president after declining an offer by Virginia Governor Douglas Wilder to serve as president of that state's community college system.

Before I could even consider Cartwright's proposal, a Cuyahoga official, Paul Shumaker, called to gauge my interest in the job. He scheduled an appointment in Cleveland and asked for a brief written statement outlining my experiences.

During the visit, I met with the search committee (much to my surprise), Cuyahoga administrators, and Thornton. Then I was ushered to a board of trustees meeting, where I was welcomed by one trustee, Rubie McCullough, as the Metropolitan Campus President. You can imagine my confusion. There were no salary or contract negotiations. There was no vetting at the campus level nor meeting with community members. This search process for a president was far different from what I had observed or was told about. But I had a plan. I thanked the board and Thornton, and decided upon my return to Winston-Salem to send them a note thanking them for their hospitality and respectfully declining their offer.

My plan was dashed in the manner described by Robert Burns: "The best laid plans of mice and men often go awry." After the board meeting, Cuyahoga's chief administrative officer, Frank Reis, apologized for the confusion. He then officially offered me the position as he talked glowingly and proudly about the future possibilities of the college under Thornton's leadership. I responded that I would let him know of my decision soon.

The next day, I met with my then-WSSU-boss. He happened to be in possession of an article from that day's edition of the Winston-Salem Journal newspaper announcing my appointment at Cuyahoga! He was upset. I had not apprised him of my interest in another job. And, why would I? It was only an exploratory visit. However, he promised something in that meeting that quickly made me accept the offer from Cuyahoga: If I stayed at WSSU, he would support me as his successor. This declaration came from a very personable and supportive man. But he was someone whose leadership was under review by the University of North Carolina General Administration President, William Friday, who had sent a representative to the college to assist him with his responsibilities.

Before I arrived officially at the Metropolitan Campus, my intuition was to visit it to understand it's physical layout and to speak with students about their experiences without divulging my identity. It was to be an important precursor to my arrival. As I began my visit, I was approached by Dr. Carol Franklin, a member of the staff who asked, because I must have appeared disoriented, if she could assist me. Then she immediately recognized me as the new campus president. Wishing to be transparent, I shared with her my plans for the day and she proceeded to escort me on a two-hour long tour that encompassed brief conversations with students, faculty, and staff.

The coincidence with Franklin and the conversations with campus constituents were fortuitous. It made me appear as an individual who valued input and consensus. I would rely on these encounters to help me succeed in my first presidency. That visit also helped me gain additional clarity about how to craft strategic priorities for the campus which were aligned with Thornton's vision for the entire college.

In April 1993, I arrived at Cuyahoga's Metropolitan Campus. It was surrounded by public housing whose residents yearned for a better life but needed help in making their desires a reality. At that time, the campus physically was a fortress, and it may have sent a message that its occupants were unwilling to reach out into the neighborhoods.

This perception was far from reality. Instead, I discovered colleagues who were more than willing to connect in the community. And that's when I knew I had made the right choice. Cuyahoga was a perfect fit. My colleagues were receptive of my leadership and I learned from my successes and failures. Thornton, without her knowing it, was a perfect role model.

## The community college legacy

With an illustrious history dating back more than 100 years, the community college as an institution has provided ready access to college for individuals from varied backgrounds. In its earlier days, the community college was often referred to as a junior college, with the goal of facilitating student transfer to four-year institutions. Eventually, its mission evolved to include the purpose of training individuals for the workforce, especially during the Great Depression. Following World War II, the G.I. Bill created educational opportunities for veterans and subsequently led to additional growth opportunities for community colleges. Public access increased due to the 1947 Truman Commission, which proposed a network of affordable public two-year institutions in states throughout the nation.

Later, an important action to increase community college access during the 1960s and '70s was the passage of the Higher Education Facilities Act of 1963. It was enacted by President Lyndon Johnson as a part of his Great Society movement, which focused on poverty, the environment, and education. Among other things, the law called for doubling college enrollment, helping to build technical institutions to close the gap in the "crucial area of trained manpower," expanding student loans, and constructing between 25 and 30 community colleges each year.

The expansion of community colleges reaffirmed the connection between education and American prosperity. Central to this notion is the community college "open door" policy, which not only gives nearly unfettered access to college but also makes available remedial courses and support services that, when accessed, are an important option for people seeking to advance educationally and economically to experience the American Dream.

Today, there are 1,108 two-year institutions across the United States, according to the American Association of Community Colleges (AACC). In 2014, 12.3 million individuals attended classes at these colleges—enabling them to transfer to four-year institutions or move into jobs of their choice. Between 85 and 90 percent of the graduates remain in their communities, contributing to the tax base and advancement of neighborhoods. The primary student population of community colleges is 49 percent white, 22 percent Hispanic, and 14 percent African-American. More than one-half of the minorities enrolled in higher education attend community colleges.

During my 11 years as the Metropolitan Campus President, we created programs to screen and refer preschool children to developmental services; established computer laboratories in newly constructed public housing and existing high schools throughout the city; and created the High Tech Academy (HTA). The HTA was the first public school established at a Cleveland college that allowed talented high school students to experience academic life, consider career choices in technology, and take classes that led to accumulated credits or degrees. We formed ties with business leaders, like former Executive Chairman and CEO of National City Bank, now PNC, David Daberko, and public officials, including the current mayor of Cleveland, Frank Jackson, who at the time was a city councilman.

Today, under one of my successors, Dr. Michael Schoop, the Metropolitan Campus is an exuberant and supportive environment where students are educated and, where necessary, provided with personal support to mitigate many of the challenges that interfere with their educational pursuits. It is an attractive and inviting learning environment, and its latest construction project, a new Campus Center, will undoubtedly bring in more students and community members.

Early in my tenure at Cuyahoga, I applied for a few other presidencies. I was granted several first-round interviews and twice was selected as a finalist. You may not land a presidency or leadership post immediately, even when you possess one. And so, I learned if you do not obtain the job you seek, ask for feedback from the search committee or firm that would be beneficial as you prepare for upcoming job searches.

In February 2004, an opportunity presented itself and I left Cuyahoga for the chancellorship of Delgado Community College in New Orleans, Louisiana. I was not actively seeking a position. Instead, I was courted by the firm handling the search. Just before my appointment was announced, however, the leader of the faculty organization at Delgado received an anonymous letter alleging that I unfairly discharged an employee and was attempting to "turn the Metropolitan Campus black," whatever that means.

Dr. Walter Bumphus, then-president of the Louisiana Community and Technical College System (LCTCS), recognized this allegation was preposterous. At the time, 60 percent of the Metropolitan Campus student body was African-American. Some members of the search committee still believed the letter was a deeply-seeded revelation of shortcomings in my leadership. But Bumphus' response was ingenious, he invited members of the committee to journey to Cleveland, tour the Metropolitan Campus and talk with individuals familiar with me and my leadership capabilities.

During the visit, they met with the mayor of Cleveland, Jane Campbell, numerous business leaders, and several of my colleagues. According to Bumphus, who subsequently offered me the job the following day, every visitor left favorably impressed.

It may sound strange, but I actually benefitted from the search committee's hesitation. The trip made them realize what my presence might mean to the college and community. This realization helped create a more favorable environment for launching my work at Delgado and confronting the unusual political structure in Louisiana. And unusual it was.

In Cleveland, for example, the business community worked with public officials to complete important economic development projects. These included lakefront revitalization, which led to development of the Rock and Roll Hall of Fame, the Great Lakes Science Center, and the new Browns football stadium. Collaboration between the public and private sector also occurred on the Gateway project, which led to the completion of a new basketball arena for the Cleveland Cavaliers and a new baseball field for the Cleveland Indians. The opposite was evident in New Orleans, as collaboration between public and private sectors was infrequent.

**The politics of a natural disaster**

Because the political system in Louisiana was highly centralized in the state capital of Baton Rouge, it necessitated institutions have relationships with the powerful legislative delegations to secure vital funding for programs and facilities. There were four systems and boards representing higher education that competed for scarce resources: Louisiana State University, the University of Louisiana, Southern University, and the LCTCS, headed by Bumphus.

The highly centralized state system of government was tested during the aftermath of Hurricane Katrina. There was disagreement and contention among federal, state, and parish (the equivalent of counties) officials on how to provide relief—especially to those residents who were stranded in New Orleans. The rancor that ensued between the parties possibly delayed the immediate delivery of aid to New Orleans' residents, those from other parishes, and the overall recovery efforts.

Despite the political, environmental, and personal challenges caused by the storm, we realized a top priority was helping students return to Delgado and the city—both severely damaged by the storm.

A new emergency response plan was necessary for the college that involved individuals who had no previous administrative experience, since many of our executives could not join us immediately at the emergency headquarters located on the campus of Baton Rouge Community College. We set out to restore IT functions, launch a communications plan, locate and communicate with students, and develop a schedule for remediating buildings where we could. The faculty and staff stalwartly recruited and enrolled students. And I worked with LCTCS officials to secure $40 million to keep some of our colleagues employed and to renovate facilities. Bumphus himself held statewide facilities overseers—who were concerned about our efforts to reopen the college—in abeyance until 10,002 of the 17,500 students who attended Delgado prior to Hurricane Katrina re-enrolled.

To this day, I continue to be very proud of my Delgado colleagues and friends who assumed significant responsibilities far beyond what they were accustomed to doing following the hurricane. Among them is Debbie Lea, a program director who ultimately became the chief academic officer and, upon my departure, the acting chancellor. She led the college through a successful re-accreditation process with the Southern Association of College and Schools (SACS). Debbie and her husband, Scott, sustained damage to their home in New Orleans, her automobile was destroyed during Katrina, and its replacement was totaled during Hurricane Rita in Baton Rouge after they relocated there.

I am also proud of Thomas Lovince, the Chief Information Officer, who led his colleagues, escorted by a Louisiana highway patrol car, from our temporary enclave at Baton Rouge Community College to New Orleans. They were on a rescue mission whose purpose was to recover files—student records in particular—before the battery life expired on the backup computers at our redundancy site on the seventh floor of the Louisiana State University Health Sciences Center, which was still surrounded by water seven days after the hurricane. They retrieved the files, but the data appeared to be corrupted. Lovince and his staff worked tirelessly, applying every technology remedy available to them until all files were recovered. If the student records, particularly transcripts, had not been recovered we would have ceased to exist as a college, literally.

During the recovery, I also assisted with the rebuilding of New Orleans as a participant in activities of Mayor Ray Nagin's Bring New Orleans Back Commission and Governor Kathleen Blanco's Louisiana Recovery Authority (LRA).

When Bumphus left in 2007 for a distinguished professorship and department chair at the University of Texas at Austin, I applied to be his successor. After the LCTCS board's deliberations—and a very close vote—they chose someone else.

## A precedent set in Pittsburgh

In April 2008, I left Delgado for the presidency of the Community College of Allegheny County. I packed a lot oflearning into my four years at the helm of Delgado that would be useful at Allegheny. I became the first president of African-American descent at the college and was humbled that the college, community, and board would take this unprecedented step. It occurred following the appointment of Mike Tomlin as head coach of the beloved Steelers, Pittsburgh's professional football franchise, and as Barack Obama was campaigning to become our nation's president.

My stint at Allegheny was productive in many ways. My colleagues gained a sense of pride when, together, they restored public trust and respect for their efforts to graduate more students. Private and public funding was secured for long-awaited physical improvements, including a science building that was named in honor of a legendary Pittsburgh political figure of African American descent, K. Leroy Irvis.

In addition, a capital campaign goal of $30 million was exceeded by $14 million, long before its timeframe of three years was over.

These achievements came with some challenges as well.

Public funding shortfalls meant that students bore increased financial burdens. In a single year, the board of trustees and I raised tuition by 18 percent, which we were extremely reluctant to do. And I had to shut down a downtown center attended by 800 students to balance the budget. Fortunately, our nearby Allegheny Campus absorbed the students and the programs they were enrolled in.

## Return to Cuyahoga

In July 2013, I left Allegheny to assume the college presidency at Cuyahoga. It was truly a bittersweet moment. Allegheny and the people of Pittsburgh were remarkably generous to Daphne and me, but returning to Cleveland meant coming home to a community I knew intimately and an organization that, during my absence, continued to undergo deep transformation. It was gratifying, not to mention unusual, to return as the leader of an organization where you launched your leadership journey. And thus, I became Cuyahoga Community College's fourth president in its 50-year history.

Cuyahoga has a very rich history. Charles Chapman, its founding president in 1963, did the impossible in creating the college out of whole cloth. He presided over its first tax levy, first day of classes, and the construction of the first three campuses. Today, there are four campuses with a vast array of programs that serve 55,000 students annually.

Nolen Ellison, the second president, led the college to greater technological achievements and established it as a "Beacon of Hope on the Great Lakes."

And then, of course, there is Jerry Sue Thornton, who served as president of Cuyahoga for nearly half of its history. Thornton propelled the college to national prominence as a leader of innovation that enabled students to catch dreams for the future. She developed an institution of world-class facilities and unparalleled faculty and staff. Succeeding her, quite honestly, has been my hardest test. How do you follow a legend? My decision was to apply my personalized approach to leadership to improve access to Cuyahoga, increase the rate and number of graduates from the college, expand programs, and modernize and equip spaces to create centers of excellence for developing workers.

The move back to Cleveland also allowed me to be with my children and two grandbabies, Ruby and Rory, who are precious and allow me to experience some of the early developments I missed with our children, Nakia and Kim. I cherish how Ruby and Rory fit in my arms when I hug them and how their small hands feel when I hold them in mine. Ruby and I have formed a special bond by attending plays and movies together. Watching Rory at six-months-old, walking behind a toy scooter as he pushed it (and I have the video to prove it) is a memory I will treasure.

Looking back, I have been fortunate in my various leadership roles. They have been both productive and rewarding. But, as I identify the factors that contributed to my success, I find they often emanated from relationships developed personally or vicariously. Even the achievements that appear serendipitous materialized because of their proximity to circumstances involving people I know. The circumstances included experience in increasingly progressive administrative roles, particularly my presidencies. The people included supportive advisors, loyal and committed colleagues, patient Board of Trustees members, and steadfast community partners who helped make my success possible. Also, my faith has been a constant source of strength and comfort as I face the different facets of my life. My family has kept me grounded and level-headed. And I know going forward their help will be necessary.

In formulating your personalized leadership approach, it is helpful to ponder how early events you recall—and those intimated by others—influenced you as a person and, ultimately, as a leader. For me, it was the personal connection with events of the civil rights movement that unfolded before me as a youth and young adult. The process of discovery is illustrated in the following chapter, Connecting the Fundamentals of the Personalized Approach. This chapter provides the context for the rest of *Change the Lapel Pin*, which focuses on the Three Essentials of Leadership, along with natural ability, select competencies, and on the job development.

# III. Connecting the Fundamentals of the Personalized Approach

*"I love the interrelatedness of things."*
*Terry Tempest Williams*

L eadership approaches are not boxed sets of applications which are neatly shelved then pulled down when you need them. It's better to think of these approaches as an accumulation of interrelated experiences and skills that serve as the foundation for your current responsibilities and future growth. This integration is one of the essential cornerstones of the Change the Lapel Pin model. To aid your deeper understanding of this model, and to help you develop your personalized approach, I offer the following diagram to illustrate the interrelated nature evident in *Change the Lapel Pin*. It will be the basis of my discussion from this point forward in the book.

*Leadership approaches are not boxed sets of applications which are neatly shelved then pulled down when you need them.*

# Three Essentials of Leadership

**TRAITS**
Abilities identified, strengthened, and applied that stem from Motivation, Temperament, Dominance and Aptitude.

**EDUCATION**
Knowledge derived from formal education, professional development, colleagues and other sources.

**THREE ESSENTIALS OF LEADERSHIP**

**PERSONALIZED APPROACH TO LEADERSHIP**

**EXPERIENCE**
Expertise and perspectives gained from life, work and other encounters.

**COMPETENCIES**
Skills to lead during the initial appointment, while engaging and assessing the organization and when applying cultural attributes to facilitate success.

**EXPOSURE**
Characteristics and behaviors derived from observations and interactions with people and events.

**OTHER CONSIDERATIONS**
Additional attributes and abilities, such as managing as leader, looking like a leader, recognizing and responding to challenges, honoring diversity and developing yourself and your colleagues for the future.

# Features of the Personalized Approach to Leadership

In the midst of personalizing your leadership approach, it is helpful to examine in the Three Essentials of Leadership all those pivotal incidents and moments in your life that affected you either personally or professionally. Any knowledge gained through education and training, experience converted to practice, and characteristics gleaned from people and events are examples of the possible outcomes of your examination.

Next, contributing to your personalized approach are natural traits (or capacities) that can be nourished and enriched to make your leadership unique. These abilities are most often recognized by others around you, show up in your relationships with people, or appear in the form of academic achievement. They are, however, essentially raw talent unless they are identified, cultivated, and honed through practice, work experience, and continuing education.

The Three Essentials and talent alone are not sufficient to develop and succeed as a leader. You must be technically competent. Establishing your presence early is important through clear indication that you are the one who will, with the involvement of others, lead the organization to the next level. Relating to individuals and including them in creating a framework for the organization's operation, success, and advancement must be incorporated in your leadership approach.

Assessing and managing the culture is a skill that allows you to value the contributions of others, portray transparency and accountability, adapt the organization to the needs of stakeholders, and communicate the organization's status, aspirations, and progress.

And finally, there are the unique attributes that distinguish you as a leader. Some of these encompass both style and substance and are important to fully packaging your leadership approach.

For example, do you have the ability to demonstrate your technical competence and simultaneously relate to individuals throughout the organization by managing a project? At Cuyahoga, I meet regularly with select committees and teams to demonstrate my commitment to these activities, and offer advice and direction where warranted.

How is your behavior during challenges? Do you exude a calm demeanor publicly to ensure your associates that you are equipped to handle such matters personally and to lead a response to them? This is one of the lessons I was reminded of during Delgado's challenges with Hurricane Katrina.

Do you take care to ensure that you look and sound like a leader? Sometimes being a leader requires a wardrobe upgrade, coupled with coaching to enhance your speech delivery. You never cease being a leader—the one in charge—so try to maintain a neat appearance even while shopping or even exercising.

Do you show concern for the legacy of the organization by focusing on current operations and future advancements in a global society? Do you regularly create a sense of urgency to motivate individuals? Do you engage in ongoing professional development individually and provide it for your associates?

Do you both honor and recognize the benefits of a diverse and inclusive workforce as a powerful reminder that acknowledging, understanding, accepting, valuing, and celebrating differences among people is healthy and rewarding for promoting social equality and business?

In the next few chapters, each feature of the chart will be presented in fuller detail.

# IV. Charting the Three Essentials of Leadership

In the first sections of this book, I sought to provide personal context to the Three Essentials of Leadership and explain how they helped shape my approach. As you dig deeper into the characteristics of the Three Essentials, it might be helpful if you view my perspectives on education, experience, and exposure as an example of how you might approach your individual assessment in these areas.

## EDUCATION
*Definition: Knowledge derived from formal education, professional development, colleagues and other sources.*

Phil Hinson and Anthony Sturgess, authors of *Uncommon Leadership*, believe the heart of leadership is the idea of building a core of knowledge that becomes an essential part of your expertise through the following:

Know your business. There is no substitute for being a student of the business you are in.

Know your profession. What are the critical areas of knowledge in your discipline that you need to know?

Know your customers. Be in close contact with customers, and find out as much as you can about why they deal with your organization.

Know your colleagues. Build effective relationships—with those who work for you, as well as a wider network within the organization.

So, the first of the Three Essentials of Leadership, education, is an important foundation for establishing and developing your leadership approach. A college degree is evidence, in part, that you have mastered some of the technical competencies or meet one of the qualifications for a leadership role. The professional development opportunities you undergo now and in the future are also important, as they equip you for some of the succinct aspects of the job.

My own early professional development included a fellowship program with the American Council on Education (ACE), which provided a broader understanding of how higher education institutions are organized and administered. My stint at Harvard University's Institute for Executive Management considered more specific topics, such as strategic planning, financial and budget management, and personnel development. I also attended the League for Innovation's Executive Leadership Institute, which was focused solely on preparing you for a community college presidency.

Beyond these, my different presidencies have offered numerous opportunities to learn from my colleagues on how to confront common challenges. I have contributed to these solutions, too, by sharing innovations that I applied at the colleges I have led.

Most of the dialogue between presidents occur at national meetings of organizations like the American Association of Community Colleges (AACC) and the League for Innovation. These professional associations employ commissions and committees that recommend how organizations can accomplish their strategic priorities, such as diversity and inclusion. My involvement with AACC and the League has been in many capacities, including as a member of their boards. I have also served on the boards of the Association of American Colleges and Universities (AAC&U) and ACE. Each of these provided valuable educational opportunities, as well as expanded perspectives on the development and implementation of leadership.

Outside the professional realm, leaders often have ample opportunities to get involved in their local communities, contributing their time, talent, energy, and treasure to activities and organizations that have a lasting impact. Throughout my career, I have been privileged to serve on myriad boards that represent the interests of individuals from all walks of life. Among these are United Way organizations in Pittsburgh, Pennsylvania, and Cleveland, Ohio, whose commitments to youth, families, individuals with special needs, and older Americans coincide with my own personal and professional interests.

A leader's participation in community affairs can also have a positive impact on their organization. For example, during 2017, through its Jack, Joseph, and Morton Mandel Humanities Center—funded by a $10 million gift from the Mandel Foundation—Cuyahoga led and coordinated, with 76 community and business groups, a yearlong commemoration of the 50th Anniversary of Carl B. Stokes, the first African American mayor of a major U.S. city, the career of his brother, Congressman Louis Stokes, and Cleveland's contributions to the National Civil Rights Movement. The project was designed to help establish lasting policies to improve communities economically and socially, as well as identify and train leaders to take on this responsibility in the future. As a tribute to the Stokes brothers and Cleveland, a permanent exhibit, paid entirely by private donations, was erected at the Western Reserve Historical Society's Cleveland History Center in November, 2017.

## EXPERIENCE
*Definition: Expertise and perspectives gained
from life, work, and other encounters.*

The second of the Three Essentials of Leadership is
experience. It certainly includes your ascension through
various jobs and the knowledge accrued in the process.
This is often referred to as "progressing through the ranks."
With few exceptions, in higher education most presidents
come through the academic pathway—often beginning as
a faculty member, followed by a department chairmanship,
a deanship, a vice presidency, and then a presidency. This
progression, and the knowledge gained throughout the
journey, along with the various continuing education
opportunities, often prepare you to compete for a presidency.

There are also specific experiences that shape your
leadership approach. The one which was most instructive to
me, and that I will describe in more detail later in the book,
is my bout with Hurricane Katrina. The lessons learned from
this episode transformed me into a more tactical, deliberate,
patient, and sensitive leader.

Looking back, it seems I have been working all my life. I
remember my first job at age 11, bagging groceries in a New
York neighborhood grocery store, FEDCO, for tips. I shined
shoes on Times Square and 42$^{nd}$ Street, before the glitter and
activity it now exudes, and worked in a barber shop brushing
off customers and sweeping up hair. And, as I mentioned,
when I was 14 years old I worked in a summer program for
youth funded by President Lyndon Johnson's War on Poverty.
The small earnings from these jobs was liberating, but
the work in the youth program, especially, provided more

satisfaction. I was rewarded by connecting with the children and inspired by the senior counselors—all college students—who first planted the dream of a college education in my head.

As I mentioned earlier, another experience instrumental in shaping my leadership approach is a personal one: my segregated childhood in Concord, North Carolina.

Even in this environment of separation and exclusion, my parents, James and Betty Davis, taught me to gain equality I must first respect work and persevere. My maternal grandparents, Willie and Marion Johnson, encouraged me to strive for educational attainment that would lead to a livelihood. And, above all else, to apply what I learned in the classroom, in the crucible of work, and beyond to become an active citizen committed to causes that improve the lives of my neighbors.

This is even more critical during our nation's current period of divisiveness and upheaval. Creating the new generation of leaders depends on empowered, responsible individuals with dreams bigger than themselves, who not only live in their communities but also live for their communities.

## EXPOSURE
*Definition: Characteristics and behaviors
derived from observations and
interactions with people and events.*

The last of the Three Essentials of Leadership is exposure. Over time, I have observed the characteristics of many professionals in my field and other sectors. Admittedly, there has been some behavior I would never model. Others, however, exhibited superior qualities I admired and wished to emulate. Both cases served as models of what to do and what not to do.

For example, early in my career I sought to incorporate the communication skills of the late Walter Leland Cronkite, who served as anchorman of CBS Evening News from 1962 to 1981. Cronkite reported on events during his career that challenged and heralded America, including wars, assassinations, and space travel. He was a trusted face and voice who believed in the equality of all people. Cronkite famously said, "There is no such things as a little freedom. Either you are all free or you are not free."

I was privileged to know the late Congressman Louis Stokes for more than 20 years before his death. Referred to as "The Gentleman from Ohio," which not-so-coincidentally was the title of his autobiography, Stokes served in the U.S. House of Representatives from 1969 to 1999. His remarkable life epitomizes how to overcome adversity. From the stigma of growing up in inner-city Cleveland, Ohio, to the sting of racially charged political environments across America, Stokes had a distinguished career as a congressman that included chairing committees that investigated the assassinations of President John F. Kennedy and Dr. Martin Luther King, Jr. He carried out his responsibilities with great enthusiasm and zeal at the highest level and always on behalf of the people of Cleveland whom he served. Stokes' steadfast determination and genuine humility are traits I admire and attempt to apply to my own life as I carry out my daily responsibilities.

Finally, a person I respect for his skills of persuasion—and whom you will read more about in the book—is William Clyde Friday, President Emeritus of the University of North

Carolina General Administration. His effort to desegregate the state's public, four-year universities amid a federal court order was considered an historic accomplishment.

**Charting your most pivotal moments**

As you weigh the outcomes of your own personal assessment in the Three Essentials, start identifying how they serve as the basis for your personalized leadership approach and as you perform your duties. Applying this standard may uncover a handful of vivid examples that dramatically directed the course of your life and work. In recounting these examples, it should be abundantly clear how you were enriched (or diminished) at the time. Did your behavior immediately change? What has been the impact on your career choice? Has this contributed to your path toward and ideals about leadership?

On the following chart, I want you to describe the really important events in the Three Essentials of Leadership—education, experience, and exposure—that have impacted your personal attributes, career choices, and leadership approach. The effects in each of these areas are often entwined and non-sequential. Record three or four in each element, and at the end of the exercise, summarize how they individually and collectively contribute to your leadership journey. Save the results as a baseline for comparing your eventual growth and advancement.

## Charting Events from the Three Essentials

| INCIDENT | IMPACT | | |
|---|---|---|---|
| Description | Personal | Career Choice | Leadership Approach |
| EDUCATION | | | |
| | | | |
| | | | |
| EXPERIENCE | | | |
| | | | |
| | | | |
| EXPOSURE | | | |
| | | | |
| | | | |

In the subsequent chapters, I will help you form substance
around your attributes in these areas by helping you identify
natural abilities and providing you with an understanding
of the complementary skills and competencies that will
contribute to your success. Also, it is important not to
abandon reliance on education, experience, and exposure as
the basis for your continued growth and development as a
leader. These assets are indispensable to helping you create
the full-range of abilities needed for success during your
leadership journey.

# V. Understanding and Applying the Origins of Leadership

*Abilities identified, strengthened,
and applied, that stem from
Motivation, Temperament,
Dominance, and Aptitude.*

Natural abilities often emerge early and are constituted by passionate commitment and conviction, most often to people and causes. Let's consider that former Secretary of State, First Lady, and presidential candidate Hillary Clinton is among the many leaders who I believe fit this definition.

On a trip to Chicago with her youth ministry, Clinton witnessed a speech delivered by Dr. Martin Luther King Jr. which sparked lifelong passion for social justice and public service. At Wellesley College, she became a prominent student leader who was selected to be the first student speaker at the commencement ceremony. After college, she enrolled and completed Yale Law School, where she was one of just 27 women in her graduating class.

After law school, Clinton went to work for the Children's Defense Fund going door-to-door in New Bedford, Massachusetts, gathering stories about the lack of schooling for children with disabilities. This commitment to public service and fighting for others—especially children and families—has stayed with her throughout her life. She co-founded Arkansas Advocates for Children and Families and helped create the federal Children's Health Insurance Program (CHIP), which provides health coverage to more than 8 million children annually.

In examining the natural sources of leadership and how they are nurtured to produce competent leaders, scientists Andrew King, Dominic Johnson, and Mark Van Vugt argued that across species individuals are more likely to emerge as leaders if they have a particular trait—ancient roots and evolutionary origins—that increase their propensity to act first in solving problems that aid the survival and nourishment of a species. Their assessment, published as "Origins and Evolution of Leadership," gets to the heart of the origins of leadership, concluding that motivation, temperament, dominance, and aptitude are among the key properties that may be seen individually and collectively in great leaders.

Motivation is one of the traits that, when used by individuals to reach a destination, can direct group behavior. Thus, leadership in an organization is often determined by whoever has the greatest incentive to move it, which correlates strongly with traits associated with ambition and autonomy. This trait is described by Heather Fork in *What Are Your Natural Gifts? Is Your Job Making the Most of Them?* as goal-focused, characterized by ambitions for the organization and self. Competent and confident are distinctions of this trait, along with adaptability. Motivated leaders can attract followers and are viewed as role-models. But sometimes they can be so focused on moving the organization forward that they leave individuals behind as they forge ahead.

Next, the temperament of leaders often inspires faithful followers because of the personal connection made with others. Fork suggests this trait exudes loyalty to the organization and to the self, making leaders dutiful and committed.

They promote collaboration, which is an important requirement for the current workforce along with trustworthiness and a commitment to ethical standards. Leaders with a good temperament are level-headed and extremely well-prepared because of persistent hard work and long hours. On occasion, leaders with this attribute may be perceived as lacking motivation and having low levels of energy, even being considered boring.

Dominance correlates highly with leadership emergence. Dominant members of a species sometimes take on leadership status because they operate more autonomously and hold particularly strong influence and position established within professional and social networks. This trait contributes to self-confidence and being protective of others. Dominant leaders take risks, are self-reliant, and strong-willed. Unfortunately, this last characteristic may suggest the most talkative member of a group often becomes the group's leader, regardless of the quality of that person's inputs. Additionally, this characteristic does not naturally embrace collaboration and, therefore, the leader is often diminished because their responses are based more on convenient and short-term solutions and less on strategy to advance the organization over time.

Finally, having some unique aptitude or expertise makes it more likely an individual will emerge as a leader. This fact correlates with leadership in organizations that require considerable specialized knowledge and training, like the tech industry, but not in those that require risk-taking and physical talents. These individuals are usually purposeful, conscientious, and responsible. They display a high level of confidence in their own abilities and are often frustrated when they cannot arrive at immediate answers to lingering and persistent challenges. Travis Bradberry, in "5 Boneheaded Ways Smart People Fail," believes that another shortcoming is hubris, which can lead to not considering what other people think.

As you can see, there are strengths and shortcoming in each trait when individually considered. It is important to identify them through self-assessment and feedback from thoughtful-but-candid colleagues and followers. The benefit of natural origins comes when they are applied in tandem with the Three Essentials—education, experience, and exposure—and competencies and skills developed on the job and elsewhere.

## Beyond trait leadership

Beyond the concept of trait leadership is the idea that leadership can be learned and applied—so called, "situational leadership." It is based on a theory that was developed in the mid-1970s by Paul Hersey, author of *Situational Leadership*, and Ken Blanchard, who wrote *One Minute Manager*.

Four interventions are used in the situational approach: telling, selling, participating, and delegating. Its foundation lies in teaching leaders to diagnose the needs of an individual or a team and then use the appropriate strategy to respond to the needs of the person and the situation. The leader selects the appropriate style for the situation and readiness level of the employee. Here is a more detailed look at the elements of situational leadership:

## Telling

Employees lack the specific skills required for the job in hand and are unable and unwilling to take responsibility for this job or task.

**Intervention:** Is characterized by one-way communication in which the leader defines the roles of the individual or group and provides the what, how, why, when, and where to do the task.

## Selling

Employees are unable to take on responsibility for the task being done; however, they are willing to work at the task.

They are novice but enthusiastic.

**Intervention:** While the leader is still providing direction, he or she is now using two-way communication and providing the socio-emotional support that will allow the individual or group being influenced to buy into the process.

## Participating

Employees are experienced and able to do that task but lack the confidence or willingness to take on responsibility.
**Intervention:**This is shared decision-making about aspects of how the task is accomplished. The leader provides fewer task behaviors while maintaining high relationship behavior.

## Delegating

Employees are experienced at the task and comfortable with their own ability to do it well. They are able and willing to not only do the task, but to take responsibility for it.
**Intervention:**The leader is still involved in decisions; however, the process and responsibility has been passed to the individual or group. The leader stays involved to monitor progress.

Since leadership is a combination of factors, including education, experience and exposure, both trait and situational leadership have attributes that can be applied to develop one's leadership style.

First, with respect to trait leadership origins of motivation, temperament, dominance, and knowledge, most individuals possess these characteristics in varying degrees. Leaders must recognize not only their existence, but also when each characteristic emerges and how it is applied as a strategy.

Next, in cases of situational leadership, where an

individual is new to an organization or a new initiative is introduced, specific direction may be required to adequately engage in telling and selling. But as the individual and organization mature, the use of participating and delegating stages is required to advance any organization forward.

My purpose here is not to present an exhaustive discussion of either trait or situational leadership. That is far beyond the scope of this book. But, since I contend leadership is a combination of factors, I believe both trait and situational leadership have attributes that can be applied to develop one's leadership style.

Like the "Level 5 Leader," described by author Jim Collins in *Good to Great: Why Some Companies Make the Leap and Others Do Not*, effective leaders understand how to apply elements of both leadership types. They fortify their natural attributes, as in trait leadership, and gain experience on how to apply leadership in specific instances, like in situational leadership.

Often, the experienced leader has an advantage in this regard. These individuals have been able to develop, sometimes through trial and error, in a manner that provides them constructive feedback on how to strengthen their leadership skills.

The novice leader can learn much from this example. Understandably, their technical expertise in the leadership role is also important. The ability to present a vision, devise and implement the strategies and plans to carry it out, and build step-by-step on successes are important. But being astute technically at something doesn't necessarily mean you are able to deliver results that include the nuances that separate good from great.

Whether you are an experienced leader or one new to your role, the combination of trait and situational leadership can be constructive because it can be applied by people at all levels in all types of organizations. Following are some examples of characteristics that will aid in your development in this arena.

### Commanding demeanor

A commanding demeanor is often associated with accomplished leaders. Terms sometimes used to describe these individuals are motivated, inspired, and polished. And a neat, stylish appearance can possibly accentuate the image they have developed over time because of repetition and consistency in representing and articulating the organization's vision, core values, and operational principles. For new leaders, a professional development course that incorporates public speaking lessons can offer a head start on developing the mannerisms necessary in the leadership role.

### Consistent messaging

An ally to a commanding demeanor is consistent messaging. Done properly, it is perhaps one of the most powerful tools a leader can possess. Why? Because it allows for presenting in a few words what the organization strives to accomplish, how it can be done, and by whom.

For example, I have shared with you that as a college president, among my major responsibilities is graduating more students each year within a specific timeframe in accordance with national standards. Among these standards is the Integrated Postsecondary Education Data System (IPEDS) which is mandatory for colleges participating in any federal assistance program authorized by Title IV of the Higher Education Act of 1965. To comply with IPEDS, the student experience during the all-important first year is important for getting students on track to graduate more quickly and in higher numbers. I use the term "success and completion" to symbolize the mandatory student programs, intrusive tutoring, advising and counseling, and internships that connect students to the college, moving them towards graduation and, subsequently, four-year institutions or the workforce. This work is carried out by individuals at every level of the college.

Consistent messaging is also a way you assert your hopes and aspirations for the organization. It allows others to embrace a common vision, know the direction of the organization, and understand how all work is valued and contributes to successful outcomes. In this context, the culture of the organization transforms to incorporate the language emphasized in the leader's message. Author E.D. Hirsch popularized this phenomenon as cultural literacy; the ability to understand and participate fluently in a given (organizational) culture.

### Acting and doing
Consistent messaging can be modeled. The term that comes to mind here is "walking the talk," where you demonstrate beliefs through actions and deeds. Sometimes, this is represented by reallocating resources to fund initiatives. Another way to build support for the message is to connect with individuals throughout the organization to seek and use their advice and recommendations.

Providing periodic updates through public appearances, such as town hall meetings, publications, and social media, shows commitment to an agreed-upon course of action. In addition to other forms of communications, including newsletters and blogs, I operate a college-supported Twitter account that is useful for notifying the college community of my professional involvements throughout and away from the campus.

Your physical presence both inside and outside the organization can more firmly establish your identity. Being active in professional organizations provides an opportunity to learn from and contribute to the global dialog about running an organization. Involvement in other networks created through social and business interactions, such as non-profit boards, provides further enrichment and exposure.

## Observant

Besides "acting and doing," being observant is one of the most important attributes you can possess. Noticing details and recognizing patterns can help you be proactive in addressing challenges and responding to trends.

The result of being an observant leader is understanding, what President Emerita of Kent State University, Carol Cartwright, calls the "rhythm of the organization." This heightened awareness takes time to develop, but when established allows leaders to discern what is there, what they expect to be there and to notice what is missing. It is discerning the heart of the organization, its tempo and energy, and perceiving where it may be out of synch.

So how do you develop all these capabilities? First, experience is often a key element to becoming observant. Individuals who go through the cycle of leadership, such as creating a vision, introducing strategic priorities, assessing their effectiveness, and scaling the outcomes deepens understanding of how the organization will respond to such future activities. (I discuss these elements in greater detail in the next chapter when introducing the Uninterrupted Cycle of Leadership Effectiveness or UnCLE.)

Next, understanding people is essential to becoming a

more observant leader. Discerning what motivates them, discovering their preferred communication methods, and why they are succeeding, or not, helps the leader establish a baseline so when irregularities occur, you identify them more readily.

Once you can understand people, it's imperative to create stronger personal connections that allow you to feel comfortable in open and honest dialogue. This may later help uncover misunderstanding and defuse conflict. In the process, individuals believe their point of view has been heard. Besides this benefit, other important outcomes are trust and respect in an atmosphere of problem-solving and improved teamwork.

Finally, demonstrate being observant through active listening—concentrating on what is being said by using verbal and non-verbal messages, such as maintaining eye contact, nodding your head, smiling, and encouraging the speaker to continue. By providing this feedback, the person speaking will usually feel more at ease and, perhaps, communicate more easily, openly, and honestly.

One last point, organizations are easily unnerved. Sometimes a small adjustment or action can hamper productivity and morale. It is important, then, for the leader to remain vigilant about staying in touch with people. This has been referred to as "healthy paranoia," a sort of intuition honed through the methods cited above. These will make the leader more observant and equipped for most eventualities.

To recap, the question of whether leaders are born or made is a constant reminder of the complexities associated with the origins of leadership. Erika Andersen, after observing and interviewing thousands of people in business for her article "Are Leaders Born or Made?", concluded that leadership capability falls along a bell curve.

The folks at the very far right of the leadership bell curve start out very good and tend to get even better as they go along. Then there are the folks at the very far left of the curve that no matter how hard they try, are simply never going to be very good leaders. Finally, there's the big middle of the curve, where the vast majority of us live. And that's where the real potential for "made" leaders lies.

So, while I believe that leadership is undoubtedly rooted in natural origins that have been linked to the survival of certain species, including humans (as Andersen suggests), these attributes must be nourished through ongoing training in systems of professional development. But, neither talent nor training are sufficient to produce the well-rounded leader.

Also required are certain personal qualities that accentuate natural ability and education. Among these is a commanding demeanor that motivates and inspires your employees. Your team needs to view you as a constant. Your messages and actions must be consistent to promote knowledge and understanding of your leadership approach and the direction for the organization. These actions also assist you in developing a heightened awareness of the organization and the small, but important matters that serve to either derail or contribute to your leadership efforts. Your physical presence throughout the organization and beyond helps affirm your personal commitment to institutional and community advancement.

The figure that follows is an interpretation of how traits interact to contribute to your personalized leadership approach. Please note that these traits act collectively. One trait does not outrank the others, but on occasion you may rely on one or another to achieve a specific outcome, such as motivating your colleagues, depicting empathy or passion, taking charge, coming up with a solution, or responding to a crisis. Also, as the figure illustrates, natural traits comingle with the other elements of the *Change the Lapel Pin* model to create the integration essential to the formation of your enduring personalized approach to leadership.

## Interactions of Traits and Other Key Elements of the Personalized Approach

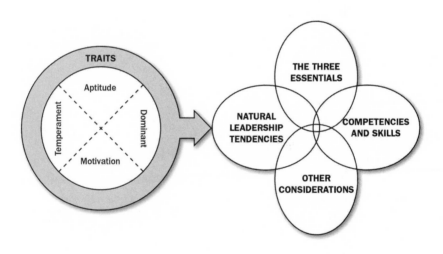

# VI. Competencies and Skills for Starting and Growing as a Leader

*Skills to lead during the initial appointment, while engaging and assessing the organization, and when applying cultural attributes to facilitate success.*

Although the tenure of college presidents is approximately six years, I have witnessed recently the dismissal of college presidents following only three to 18 months on the job—demonstrating they either were bad fits, ill-prepared for the role, or the campus community, including the Board of Trustees, was not concerned with institutional transformation.

Reasons for the terminations ranged from allegations of poor communications with the Board of Trustees, to lack of strategic planning for the college, to planning an inauguration and purchasing—supposedly without Board consent—the academic garb and regalia that usually accompanies such an event. I have also read about some college Boards that do not prepare adequately for a different leader; thus, they appear disinterested in the success of the new president and more concerned with protecting self-interests and maintaining the *status quo.*

Accordingly, the first section in this chapter is designed to ensure you do not fail during this initial period as a new leader. It describes how to prepare for leadership and the skills needed to progress in a role during the short-term. Michael Watkins, in his book *The First 90 Days*, says transitions are a critical time for leaders. Moving into a new position is the biggest challenge one will face. While transitions offer a chance to start fresh and make needed changes in an organization, they also place leaders in a position of acute vulnerability.

Glenn Llopis, author of "6 Things Wise Leaders Do to Engage Their Employees," discovered through his research that 70 percent of U.S. employees are miserable at work and or feel disengaged on the job. This is disturbing news and an indicator that leaders are having trouble finding ways to stimulate engagement with today's employees—a workforce that is much younger and more diverse.

So, next, in perhaps the most important section of the book, I will describe how to engage your workforce strategically and operationally to reach organizational benchmarks and milestones. This happens when you structure the organization to allow employees, as Llopis concludes, "to be their authentic selves so they can leverage their strengths and unique perspectives."

And finally, I outline the importance of culture as a tool to foster teamwork, increase accountability and transparency in operations, adapt to the needs of external and internal stakeholders, and communicate the status of the organization. With these elements etched in an organization's cultural ethos, it is plausible your employees can contribute systematically and incrementally to the excellence necessary to become a self-regarding organization—one that continually builds on successes to improve productivity and outcomes.

# Advice for Incoming Leaders

Your personalized approach to leadership will not be ingrained at the time of your first leadership opportunity. Experience in the role will help you greatly. It is important, however, that you begin your experience properly.

As I referenced earlier, the term "change the lapel pin," represents a paradigm shift in how new and veteran leaders operate and advance contemporary systems and organizations. I conceived the term during my second college presidency when I replaced a lapel pin with another one. The small gesture unintentionally marked my arrival and served as an opportunity to unveil my hopes and aspirations for the institution built upon the foundations of the previous president.

Physical manifestation of leadership sends a powerful message. For example, at a welcoming reception for Leonard Schaeffer as the incoming CEO for Blue Cross of California, now WellPoint Health Networks, there was a five feet tall ice sculpture carved from blue ice and artistically decorated with succulent pink prawns. When he asked where it came from, he was introduced to the company's pastry chef, who he later fired. After all, the company at that time was the worst-performing of the 77 Blue Cross plans across the country, with annual operating losses of $165 million. With the organization teetering on the edge of insolvency, ice sculpting hardly seemed like a core function. Since then, WellPoint Health Networks has transformed itself from a floundering bureaucracy into a strong public company, one of the largest health insurance organizations in the United States.

You may not have to do anything so dramatic as firing someone for your first act as a leader. But leaders who are new to an organization must be deliberate about presenting themselves, their management styles, and outlook for the organization quickly in a window of opportunity often referred to as the "honeymoon" period. This interval can last one to six months, depending on the immediate challenges and complexities of the organization, and is critical to establishing the direction of the organization and conveying immediate goals and eventual outcomes. Some college presidents present this information to various audiences during inaugurations. And there are less ceremonial ways this can happen, for example, through receptions, open seminars, town hall gatherings, and individual meetings.

During the honeymoon period, incoming leaders might identify a knowledgeable and experienced individual to serve as a coach and confidante to offer advice on how to develop interpersonal connections, guard against inertia, and introduce initiatives that constitute the next phase of the organization's growth. I have personally taken on this responsibility with several newly minted two-year college presidents. These relationships are with colleagues I have known for years and watched develop in various roles, some under my leadership.

During our coaching sessions, they tend to be accepting of recommendations on how to approach and launch their presidencies. They appreciate critical feedback on various initiatives they want to implement and understand the importance of open and honest dialog around problems and solutions. Because of this, they have established themselves and experienced success over time at their respective institutions.

**The "honeymoon" period can be critical**
Incoming leaders who do not capitalize on the honeymoon
grace period may create problems that plague them
throughout their tenure. One example is Lawrence
Summers, who in July 2001, was appointed as president of
Harvard University. This was initially viewed as a major
accomplishment. As a noted economist, Summers, a
graduate and former professor at Harvard, honored his
venerable *alma mater* through his government service,
particularly his post as secretary of the U.S. Treasury. But his
introduction to the college was controversial, which created a
litany of problems he never recovered from.

Shortly after his appointment, Summers was criticized
for accusing a black professor, Cornel West, of allegedly
missing three weeks of classes to work on the Bill Bradley
presidential campaign. Summers also complained that West
was contributing to grade inflation and claimed West's rap
album was an embarrassment to the university.

A few years later, Summers sparked controversy again.
In January 2005, while attending a conference entitled
"Diversifying the Science and Engineering Workforce,"
Summers suggested that underrepresentation of women
in science is due to aptitude and less to patterns of
discrimination and socialization.

Partly in response to this, the Harvard Arts and Sciences
graduate faculty passed a motion censuring Summers. And
in February 2006, Summers announced his intention to step
down the following June at the end of the school year.

The well-publicized Summers case is unusual. It does
suggest, however, that an initial miscue can hamper or derail
a leadership opportunity. It also underscores the fact it is the
responsibility of a new leader to understand the dynamics

of the organization he or she is joining. This understanding is developed through transactions with members of the organization that enable you to learn and connect with them. But this knowledge must also be established through incremental experiences that develop and prepare you for a leadership post.

I described this process in "Personal Pathways to the Presidency," an article I wrote for the spring 2009 issue of *The Presidency*, the magazine of the American Council on Education. The article was based on my career journey and offered advice to individuals contemplating becoming a college CEO. I believed my experience would help outline the personal and professional attributes that might benefit both prospective and current presidents.

First, and in concert with *The Presidency* article, leadership is a product of not only education and job experience, but of perspectives established through direct contact with others or during observations of how leadership is applied.

Second, you must have a stalwart commitment to your professional development. This commitment takes shape in many forms, but all help satisfy the responsibility of keeping abreast of emerging trends and issues. Leadership is further enriched through involvement in activities outside the organization that add to the understanding of global issues that impact modern-day leadership.

In *Good to Great*, Jim Collins offers another idea to symbolize these leadership evolution threads by distinguishing between Level 1 and Level 5 supervisory workers. At Level 1 is the accomplished manager who makes productive contributions through talent, knowledge, skills, and good work habits. But to become a Level 5 leader requires more. You must build enduring greatness through a paradoxical blend of personal humility and professional will. In other words, Level 5 leaders are a combination of the accomplished manager plus personal associations, attributes, and circumstances that, when combined, contribute to their viability as leaders.

### Understanding social and emotional dynamics

Your emotions will be important as you create and carry out your personalized approach to leadership. According to John Mayer and Peter Salovey, who are credited with first defining the concept, emotional intelligence is the ability to accurately perceive your own and others' emotions, to understand the signals that emotions send about relationships, and to manage your own and others' emotions. Sara Fletcher suggests in "5 Reasons Why Emotional Intelligence is Critical in Leadership" that every individual possesses different levels, but for them to become effective leaders, they need a high level of emotional intelligence.

*Your emotions will be important as you create and carry out your personalized approach to leadership.*

But because people who are strong in some of its elements can be utterly lacking in others (sometimes to disastrous effect) and because emotions are difficult to define and assess, I decided against adding emotional intelligence as one of my essential elements of leadership. Rather, I chose to focus on establishing an emotional skill set that could accentuate your abilities and serve as an overarching component of your personalized approach. So, enhancing one's interpersonal competence is very important.

To accomplish this aim, you must first understand your own social and emotional dynamics. Some experts on leadership, such as psychologist and author Daniel Goleman, might refer to this as assessing one's emotional mindset to understand behaviors that might detract from or contribute to success in the workplace. Among the many measures available for this assessment is an online program offered by Mind Tools.

The program applies principles of emotional intelligence, beginning first with self-awareness, or the ability to identify moods that affect your behavior and impact those around you. In its article "Emotional Intelligence in Leadership," Mind Tools associates suggest you spend time to reflect on your thoughts away from the organization to improve self-awareness. This reflection will help you slow down to examine why certain people and situations cause an emotional reaction and how you can appropriately react to nearly every encounter to identify an appropriate response.

Next in the Mind Tools program is self-regulation, which entails staying in touch with feelings and the influences that cause stress or anxiety. Leaders who are in control of their feelings can create an environment of trust and fairness. Leaders who can self-regulate seldom lose control of their temper when confronted by situations or individuals. You remain in charge by evaluating what response the situation warrants. You rely on values, think about the impact on your leadership, and consider where the situation occurred, in a public or private setting. Practicing being calm and allowing an initial emotional reaction can often lead to a more appropriate response.

Following self-regulation is self-motivation, which is strongly affected by emotions—when you're distracted by your emotions, you may find it hard to see tasks through. So, if there is one trait virtually all effective leaders must have, it is motivation. They must be driven to achieve beyond expectations—their own and everyone else's. Occasionally, you must determine how motivated you are as a leader. Lack of motivation can signal you are disinterested in the organization and its people. When experienced leaders find themselves in this situation, they often introduce initiatives that build upon existing success or create a new sense of urgency to drive personal and organizational renewal.

Next is empathy—relating to the ability to recognize other people's emotions and understand their perspectives in the process of making intelligent decisions. Empathy translates into putting yourself in someone else's position. This is an important tool that allows you to relate to one or multiple individuals on a personal level. Sometimes there is no recourse to an unpopular action if it is in the best interest of the organization. When this happens, you must be prepared to seek input in advance and to substantiate why the decision was necessary. In public settings, pay attention to your body language—it can reveal your emotional mindset at that moment.

And last in the Mind Tools program is social skills— the ability to build rapport. Social skills are an essential part of leadership that enable you to build good working relationships. Daniel Goleman defines social skills as friendliness with a purpose; moving people in the direction you desire, whether it is agreement on a new marketing strategy or enthusiasm about a new product. Take time to improve your social skills by learning to resolve conflict as it arises across the organization, regardless of from where it emanates. To accomplish this, you must have connections to trusted individuals that bring matters requiring your direct attention to you before they become corrosive.

Coming to grips with your emotional constitution provides a great foundation for important connections with others. You will need this skill in dealing with individuals in the organization who present a variety of dispositions and to improve organizational health—defined by Patrick Lencioni, author of *The Advantage: Why Organizational Health Trumps Everything Else in Business*, as high degrees of morale and productivity and very little turnover among employees.

Psychoanalyst and author Manfred F. R. Kets de Vries, in an interview with Diane Coutu, author of "Putting Leaders on the Couch," concludes that emotional intelligence involves a lot more than just being introspective. It also involves what he calls the "Teddy Bear Factor": Do people feel comfortable with you? Do they want to be close to you? An emotionally intelligent leader also knows how to single people out. Plus, they tend to make better team players and are more effective at motivating themselves and others.

## Jeff Bezos, emotionally intelligent boss
The force behind Amazon.com is its affable, emotionally intelligent, and driven CEO, Jeff Bezos, who possesses a quirky laugh, self-deprecating style, and is obsessed with the hearts and minds of his customers. One of his most notable quotes is "The best customer service is if the customer doesn't need to call you, doesn't need to talk to you. It just works." Bezos' long-term perspective on and understanding of relationships is the product of a legendary, natural business acumen, nurtured during his early youth on the

ranch of his maternal grandfather, Lawrence Gise. *BBCNews. com* suggested that "If the Internet was the new Rock & Roll, Jeff Bezos is its Elvis." This quote essentially sums up the fact that, like Elvis, Bezos started his career in a modest way, but was determined to seize every opportunity at success.

Amazon.com began as a bookstore in 1994 and has quickly exploded into a multi-billion-dollar enterprise that has transformed the way people shop. But, according to most online shopping experts, Amazon is just not another Internet success story—it's the standard by which web-based businesses are judged, especially by shoppers.

Today, Amazon sells more than $10 billion each year in goods and services, and its technology has influenced changes to business for decades to come. Kindle, Amazon's wireless digital reading device, gave the term "page turning" a completely new definition. After he purchased the *Washington Post*, Bezos rejuvenated it through his inimitable hands-on approach, developed when he personally responded to online orders during Amazon's early days. He founded Blue Origin, a space-flight startup. And, he launched Alexa—Amazon's unprecedented artificial intelligence voice service built in the cloud. She provides capabilities or skills that enable one to interact with devices and ask questions, among multiple other things. Alexa is always getting smarter and can adapt speech patterns, vocabulary, and personal preferences. And, Bezos' purchase of Whole Foods has some business professionals calling the acquisition ingenious, although they are still uncertain as to how it will work with the Amazon brand.

Bezos' college professors did not believe he would be a gifted leader. He was, however, a gifted student—perhaps even considered a nerd—who believed in improving the lives of individuals. This belief came from his grandfather, who once told him that "It is harder to be kind than clever." Now he applies this principle as a scientist and humanitarian to advance customer service at Amazon, to create new business opportunities with the capacity to change the world, and to develop a strategic philanthropy program to identify short- and-long-term solutions to pressing problems.

Bezos is viewed by many as a tough boss. He expects employees to continually improve customer service. The grounding for Bezos' emotional intelligence came from his grandfather, but at the heart of his belief system is a social dynamic developed while engaging with co-workers during Amazon's early days. It has become enriched through his loyalty to customers and colleagues, his ability to gain trust, and his capacity to inspire people through motivation, persistence, and success.

## Other skills to get you started

Besides presenting your aims for the organization rapidly and developing an emotional mindset for your new role, you must develop other skills that allow you to immediately face the challenges that come in a fast-paced, hyper-competitive environment. In the following sections are some examples of those skills.

**Communicating and listening.** An important tool for leaders is communication, a subject you will encounter repeatedly throughout this book. Communication skills promote clarity when conveying an organization's vision, but they also help create individual connections. To do this, you need to possess a strong, decisive voice to motivate and inspire but also understand when it is time to listen to the expressions of individuals and groups.

In this context, you must be self-aware and understand how your verbal and non-verbal communications can affect the team. Listening is an important attribute in this instance. Sara Stibitz in "How to Really Listen to Your Employees," recommends leaders eliminate distractions that imply that the person speaking and their message are unimportant. You should look for nonverbal cues, like body language, which offer deeper understanding and meaning to the conversation.

While you may find it challenging at times to control emotions, it is important to maintain poise, avoid a rush to judgment, and refrain from offering an opinion. When it is time to react, you should validate and verify the points offered by the speaker and drill down into the conversation to acknowledge what was expressed, regardless of how you feel about it.

**Collaborating and consulting.** Collaborative and consultative abilities can help recognize and reward individuals who are essential to the success of an organization. It inspires them to work toward common goals despite differences in convictions, cultural values, and operating norms. Forbes contributor and consultant Carol Kinsey Gorman maintains that such engagement is not a "nice to have" philosophy. In "8 Tips for Collaborative Leadership," she lays out the case that a collaborative and consultive approach is *essential* to productivity in an inclusive environment. She says it energizes teams, releases creativity, and makes working together both productive and joyful.

**Advocating.** Being an advocate is another important characteristic that creates an environment where colleagues feel confident and positive, thus enabling them to perform their best even under trying conditions. Professional integrity and passion are key attributes of advocacy. In this regard, you are a role model—you set the pace for the rest of the organization, creating a positive and productive working atmosphere. You inspire high, but achievable expectations and, consequently, infuse high standards of excellence in the organization.

This is an area where a vision statement can be beneficial as an aspirational, future-oriented goal for the organization. Herminia Ibarra and Morten T. Hansen posit that no company can build a coherent culture without people who either share its core values or possess the willingness and ability to embrace those values. In "Are You a Collaborative Leader?", they say that at the heart of leadership advocacy is a clearly articulated vision and values that depict where the organization expects to be and the way it pledges to serve clients, treat colleagues, and uphold professional standards.

Leadership advocacy is enhanced when unique stories about the organization are communicated. This act brings together the history of the organization and modern-day reality to create a narrative designed to elicit pride and ownership. When possible, longtime employees should be called upon to develop and deliver these accounts to achieve effective results.

### The impact for community college leaders
Community colleges offer an example of the type of organization whose leaders could be helped through this book. Each year, they serve almost 12 million students and provide an affordable and quality beginning toward

a bachelor's degree. They also play an increasingly important role in preparing individuals for good jobs. By 2020, nearly two-thirds of jobs held by Americans will require a postsecondary certificate or degree. These jobs will be created, in part, because the country has an aging workforce preparing to retire. As these individuals leave the workplace, it is anticipated the educational level of the younger generations will not enable them to immediately fill these jobs. Lawmakers, government officials, and corporate leaders see community colleges as essential in preparing the workforce for these jobs, while at the same time preparing Americans for informed, effective participation in democratic life and readying them to solve the most pressing problems of our time. And this means that leadership at the community college level has never been as important as it is today—and will be in the near-term future.

To ensure strong leadership—and an ability to fulfill the aforementioned goals—community colleges must join with other educational sectors at the school and college levels, both private and public, to prepare individuals for prosperity. In 2009, President Barack Obama announced that America cannot lead the world in the 21st century unless it has the best educated, most competitive workforce in the world. Accomplishing this aim involves increasing by 50 percent the number of Americans with a postsecondary credential, certificate, or degree by the year 2020. Painting the challenge of achieving this goal is *Time is the Enemy*, a publication by Complete College America, which reported the following:

- Of the students who begin their two-year experience in remedial education, only 9.5 percent earn an associate degree and only 13.1 percent obtain any kind degree.
- With respect to part-time students, only 7.8 percent

earn an associate degree in four years; 12.2 percent earn a one-year certificate in two years.

- Students are wasting time on access credits, on the average of 63.5 percent access credits for a 20-credit certificate and 79 percent access credits on a 60-credit associate degree.
- Average completion rates for an associate degree are 11.8 percent for low-income students, 11.1 percent for Hispanic students, and 7.5 percent for African American students.

These statistics have served as a clarion call to community college presidents and government officials at all levels to initiate long-overdue reform measures. These measures retain the open door but redesign students' educational experiences, reinvent institutional roles, and reset systems to create incentives for student and institutional success, allowing community colleges to take part in the educational and economic recovery of students. These are responsibilities with implications well beyond the two-year college environment.

Academic achievement in America has declined significantly. As a result, the current generation is in economic jeopardy unless all sectors of education work in concert to meet its needs and contribute to restoring the U.S. to a position of educational attainment that is more competitive with the world's most progressive nations.

In presenting this section of the book, my goal was to describe how to make an immediate impact as a leader and succeed during the all-important initial period. While some of this success is a result of techniques applied at the beginning of one's tenure, preparation before assuming the role is equally important. As I explained earlier, education, experience, and exposure are facets that build the foundation for leadership.

Coming to grips with your emotional mindset, as demonstrated by Jeff Bezos, provides a great foundation for connecting with people. You will need this skill set in dealing with individuals in the organization who present a variety of dispositions and to improve organizational health. Without this capacity, it is doubtful your vision will extend the depth and breadth of the organization.

Strengthening your communication to increase connections is a universal skill that can be applied in many instances and situations throughout your tenure. Collaborating and consulting can have a similar effect and, additionally, create individual relationships that build commitment and loyalty to the organization. Advocating for employees shows commitment to ensuring their interests are valued.

## Marc Byrnes, Oswald Companies

An example of this mixture of leadership characteristics is Marc Byrnes, the chairman of Oswald Companies. By all accounts, he is a successful and accomplished leader in the insurance industry whose name is synonymous with almost every economic advancement in the greater Cleveland, OH, area over the past 25 years. Downtown and neighborhood development, arts and culture revitalization, and ongoing efforts to market the city globally are areas where Byrnes' input has been invaluable.

Both his leadership and devotion to civic engagement were tested, however, when Byrnes was asked to chair the Greater Cleveland United Way Board of Trustees. It was an organization experiencing some challenges following the abrupt resignation of the previous CEO.

Although an interim CEO was identified, Byrnes recognized that this would be a brief appointment. The impending 2016 fundraising campaign provided only a short period to transform the organization and select a new CEO. He consulted both individually and collectively with influential leaders of the board and the community on perceptions of United Way. These individuals suggested the next CEO should be community-minded, principled, and inclusive, along with other traits. Byrnes showed empathy for existing staff members, but helped them understand their commitment to a culture of collaboration considering the challenges experienced by United Way.

At the organization's 2016 annual meeting, Byrnes made several important announcements. He conveyed his vision for a board structure that would expand and diversify member engagement. Disparate programs would be replaced or consolidated to direct scarce resources to the most viable ones. An aggressive annual campaign goal was announced, and two highly recognized leaders in business and civic affairs were appointed to lead the fund-raising effort. Finally, he announced the new CEO, August Napoli Jr., a well-respected, non-profit organization professional noted for his passion for Cleveland, integrity, and inclusive leadership style.

With these actions, Byrnes essentially transformed, in a matter of months, a static organization into a vibrant one. His leadership of the board through a critical time stands as an excellent example of education, experience and exposure, and working together to resolve a challenge.

Byrnes leveraged his vast experience as a leader and his

educational background, including a bachelor of arts degree from Williams College and an association with Cleveland's Center for Leadership Development. As a youth, when standing up against the discrimination of a black family that had moved next door to him in Beachwood, a suburb of Cleveland, he developed a strong resolve that he was able to draw upon in his adult life. He called on the examples of strength exhibited by his adoptive parents, Judy and Larry Byrnes, and his friend K.C. White, who has overcome extraordinary obstacles and setbacks in her battle with cystic fibrosis.

# Engaging the Organization

The previous section was essentially a primer on how you apply a personalized leadership approach to tackle a new appointment. Now that you have a baseline of how leadership emerges and is refined, let's look at how it is applied.

Organizational development is constantly studied and regularly systemized. Some systems are based on the accomplishments of one or two individuals—like Apple co-founders Steve Jobs and Steve Wozniak, pioneers of the microcomputer revolution. While Wozniak was more of a behind-the-scenes engineer, Jobs' reputation for being driven, visionary, ingenious, and sometimes enigmatic is well documented. Jobs' passion and individual effort were undeniable and important characteristics that leaders might emulate. Important also was his rarely publicized management style, where he surrounded himself with talented professionals to complement his limitations.

One example of Jobs' brilliance in minimizing his weaknesses was when he left Apple. Jobs took with him a few Apple team members with expertise in computer technology, creative design, and marketing to NeXT, a computer platform development company he founded that specialized in state-of-the-art computers for higher-education and business markets. The people who came with Jobs from Apple to NeXT had technical and creative skill sets that complemented Jobs' visionary talents.

Other forms of organizational development extol the virtues of a systematic approach. John Kotter is often referenced in this regard. Kotter is the Konosuke Matsushita Professor of Leadership, Emeritus, at the Harvard Business

School, as well as the founder of Kotter International. He has written several books, but the one that has been most impactful is *Leading Change: Why Transformation Efforts Fail* in which he describes the much-heralded, eight-step process for change management and strategy implementation.

Kotter's process begins with establishing a sense of urgency, creating a guiding coalition to respond to this urgency, and developing a vision and strategy to implement and carry out the response. The next three steps involve communicating the vision for change and soliciting and empowering broad-based action to generate short-term wins. The final two steps include consolidating gains to produce and sustain change that is anchored in new approaches in an organization's culture.

This system has become widely popular for initiating disruptive change. Among the many examples is Wesley College, a Methodist-affiliated four-year institution in Dover, Delaware, with an enrollment of 1,500 students. Wesley needed to replace a conventional core curriculum with one that reflected the needs of modern day students and society, as well as ensure the institution more easily met the standards of its regional accrediting body, the Middle States Commission on Higher Education.

School officials wanted to guard against some of the concerns that often accompanied such a monumental effort; for example, objections because it involved too many changes, it did not include the right mix of courses, it was not financially feasible, or because favorite courses were not included among the offerings.

Using the Kotter process, the college successfully transformed the core curriculum in a systematic fashion that involved feedback from all constituents. What came out of the initiative was a curriculum that now challenges and engages students and energizes faculty to teach new courses in innovative ways.

Steve Jobs and John Kotter represent different leadership styles. Jobs led organizations to new heights by emphasizing vision and timing; demonstrating passion for mission, and toiling in environments that sparked action and outcomes. These characteristics transformed his company's culture—the hardest element of an organization to shape. Kotter, on the other hand, offered a systematic, deliberate, and strategic approach which was underscored by plans, actions, and outcomes.

Capitalizing on the experiences and frameworks best represented by Jobs and Kotter can be beneficial to leaders who seek examples which can be applied in their settings. Let's take a closer look at the vision alluded to in Job's leadership approach.

**Conveying vision**

Steve Jobs' vision for Apple, to "change the world by placing a computer in the hands of everyday people," began with the first mass-produced microcomputer, the Apple II. It was followed by the first all-in-one computer, the Macintosh, and a succession of mass appeal products that included the iMac, iPod, iTunes, iPhone, and iPad.

Jobs' ideals for Apple were ambitious. But a vision should be bold. It should be a synopsis for a future organization. This type of vision is generalized, but it also undergirds the mission, which provides a more tangible framework for carrying out and weighing the effectiveness of the organization.

The vision is important because it allows you to convey

your aspirations for the organization in brief words. It should be based on a deep understanding and appreciation of global issues and perspectives. The leader's experience and demeanor can act to validate the efficacy of the vision, thus giving it greater credence as the guidepost for the organization's progress.

Kamran Akbarzadeh, author of *Leadership Soup: A Healthy Yet Tasty Recipe for Living and Leading on Purpose,* contends a vision statement should add value by inspiring action. He says when people read positive statements, it fills them with positive energy that connects them to the organization.

He suggests that to inspire this response, the vision statement must exhibit the following characteristics:

- It should be in the present tense. Vision refers to visualizing the future and painting it in the present.
- It should be short. Lengthy vision descriptions typically lose their impact and may cause people to disconnect. Short and clear, yet rich and powerful, vision statements are easy to remember and communicate.
- It should be challenging. Powerful vision testimonies pose some challenges to motivate people for growth and achieving something bigger.
- It should be attractive. If people cannot relate themselves to the vision, it is like not having vision at all.

And I add to this collection of descriptors, that it should be measurable. Each element of the vision must be assessed to determine the extent it is being accomplished through the mission, strategic priorities, and daily operations of the organization.

**Understanding timing**

To put the vision of an organization into effect, certain elements must be considered, among them timing. Jobs understood the importance of timing to establish what I call a "cause for action" that, unless addressed proactively and aggressively, could result in missed opportunity, stifle productivity, or reinforce the *status quo*. A timely response should be aimed at identifying the challenge, creating and implementing an organization-wide response, establishing the effectiveness of the intervention, and determining how the results can guard against any future inaction.

One of the important matters for those of us leading institutions of higher education is increasing the number of graduates. This would allow America to reclaim its top-ranking in the world in degree completion after falling to fourteenth among the 34-member nations of the powerful Organization for Economic Cooperation and Development. The companion to improving degree attainment at the national level is reducing the skills gap at the state and local levels, where only six of 10 workers possess the technical training needed for modern day jobs.

Some community colleges are responding to this challenging environment with interventions that direct students through programs while also enhancing the extracurricular experience and enabling students to assume leadership roles in the college and community. In the process, these colleges are ensuring their students become strong future leaders.

But responding to challenges is not easy. This is where passionate leaders, like Steve Jobs, can make a difference. By developing a vision for change and capitalizing on timing, leaders can rally employee engagement at all levels. The approach must include a strategic process that starts with a deep understanding of the internal and external forces that could stifle productivity. The strategies identified through this exercise can lead to the development of tactics in every area of the organization, resulting in increased productivity. They will serve to direct the course of the organization for now and in the future.

### Determining strategies, tactics and outcomes through UnCLE

Both Jobs and Kotter would probably agree that vision, timing, and passionate leadership, while a good start, are not alone sufficient to improve organizational outcomes. So, let's take a more in-depth look at strategic and tactical planning.

Great leadership is often measured by the extent to which growth occurs immediately and advances significantly over time. Behind this growth is often a robust vision that is accomplished with strategies and actions created in response to the vision. The outcomes of the actions, weighed against internal and external norms and standards, are the basis for the next wave of organizational refinements and innovations.

This process encompasses what I describe as the Uninterrupted Cycle for Leadership Effectiveness, UnCLE. UnCLE is a self-propagating mechanism that you apply to obtain continuously desired outcomes that, when built upon, generate repeated success. It applies "appreciative inquiry," a form of questioning that helps distinguish what currently exists, what is working, and how it can be improved.

Here's how UnCLE works:

1. **Identify a cause for action**. What trends will disrupt our business? What impact will they have on our organization? What does the data indicate? How should we respond?

2. **Identify the strategies and tactics that address it.** What are the short-term and long-term strategies to address the sense of urgency? Do they reflect national best practices and innovations developed and applied at our organization? Are they actionable and measurable?

3. **Measure success against internal expectations and external norms and standards. Build upon the outcomes.** How do we measure success of the strategies and tactics? Do the outcomes support them? Can we celebrate and build upon the results to improve organizational capacity? What do the outcomes suggest in determining next steps?

4. **Introduce the next wave of organizational refinements and innovations.** Is our approach productive? Can we implement and sustain the outcomes? What is the next iteration of our response to the current or emerging cause for action?

The following chart depicts the elements of UnCLE and how they are interrelated:

### The Uninterrupted Cycle of Leadership Effectiveness (UnCLE)

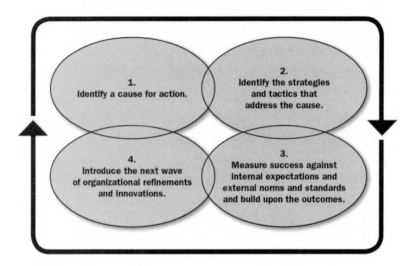

I have applied UnCLE throughout my stints as a college president. For example, my current institution's response to the increase in degree attainment requirement is focused upon improving students' access to the college and increasing their success in a learner-centered environment characterized by superior programs and services. We arrived at this "cause for action," the first step in UnCLE, based on a thorough analysis of evidence derived from data on student outcomes, including test scores and grades.

Then we asked questions. For example: What are some factors of student performance? What interventions are going to be put into place following extensive conversations with all stakeholders? How do we implement the interventions; as pilots or immediately to scale? How do we know we have been successful? At some point, will we be able to predict educational attainment based on an analysis of the performance of individual students?

We termed this approach Evidence, Inquiry, and Analytics, and it resulted in six strategic priorities: improving on-time graduation, creating a holistic student experience with more extracurricular activities, establishing more short-term workforce education programs, keeping tuition affordable, reducing the equity gap between minority and all students, and enriching the brand and image of the college.

Each of the college's three divisions—educational programs, workforce offerings, and financial and administrative services—completed tactical plans describing how they would both independently and collectively identify and establish actions to support the strategic priorities.

UnCLE emphasizes that leaders must be prepared to demonstrate the effectiveness of tactics. In the case of my institution, benchmarks were established by each division based on the model derived from the *Cleveland Clinic Way*, a book written by the Clinic's former president and CEO, Dr. Delos "Toby" Cosgrove. This book presents a model benchmark system based on national standards and best practices. The system rates services identified by patients that are important to them, measures the effectiveness of day-to-day operations, and determines the extent of the Clinic's compliance with various regulatory agencies.

The benchmarks at Cuyahoga are extensive, but the ones most critical are those that measure our progress against vanguard colleges; such as the recipients of the Aspen Prize and the Awards of Excellence from the American Association of Community Colleges (AACC). These benchmarks include graduation rates and numbers, student return rates from one semester to the next, and pass-rates in college level mathematics and English. They are the benchmarks that most effectively depict our progress against college strategic priorities and local and national norms.

When you apply UnCLE, the momentum that accrues from improved outcomes becomes an excellent opportunity to determine if the benchmarks continue to be appropriate and whether the targets promote long-term improvements. In cases where targets are surpassed repeatedly, do not increase the target because it may appear as if the rules are being changed, midstream, after they have been agreed upon. Instead, introduce alongside the targets a series of stretch goals that may serve as motivation for increased action and commitment. When targets are not attained, do not immediately change them. Rather, review the models on which they are based and assess the assumptions underlying them to determine if they continue to be appropriate and effective.

Progress on benchmarks against targets is noteworthy in the UnCLE process because the organization demonstrates its viability and the brand is enriched and serves as a powerful tool for attracting customers. In the case of Cuyahoga, employees are happy their work is contributing to increased outcomes, and efficiency and accountability are always welcomed by stakeholders—such as members of the Board of Trustees, public officials, and consumers. These are all important parties to satisfy.

What happens when outcomes are achieved? You need to capitalize on the momentum to introduce a continuing set of strategies and tactics that build upon the current iterations and frame the benchmarks and performance targets around them, just as you did previously. Now is not the time to become complacent.

Keep in mind that progress within these steps is almost never linear. Expect overlap, particularly when strategic priorities are multiple. Setbacks are a possibility. It is important, however, to review progress periodically to guard against stasis. And, on occasion, it may be necessary to simply eliminate, modify, or introduce strategies when existing ones prove ineffectual.

I provide a more thorough discussion and example of how the UnCLE model is applied in a later section of this chapter entitled "Leader as Manager to Attain Organizational Excellence."

**Building commitment**

Earlier, I described the important role at my college of administrative divisions—educational programs, workforce offerings, and financial and administrative services— and their respective leaders. The expectation for division leaders is that they individually and collectively represent the mission and vision of the college by making strategic priorities actionable. The product is a tactical plan which also ensures widespread commitment and involvement by individuals in their respective units.

In support of this aim, I introduced the President's Council as a formalized body of leaders from the faculty and staff who discuss, deliberate, and build consensus on actions for achieving goals and objectives around student achievement. Often the conventional organizational hierarchy does not allow for engagement through such a "kitchen cabinet" application. But a concerted effort *must* be undertaken to ensure your closer proximity to individuals who carry out day-to-day operations and who often know firsthand how to address specific challenges and opportunities. This is where you can gain additional respect and support by flattening the organization, either physically or perceptually, allowing you to develop stronger ties with coalitions of respected individuals who advise on important matters and represent the interests and opinions of their colleagues. Be sure to listen and respond. Emphasize that the group promotes collective engagement and not individual interests that should be addressed though existing channels.

Further, being visible and approachable provides an opportunity to be known on a personal level and display interpersonal skills that complement technical expertise.

Finally, encourage managers to apply similar approaches in their divisions and departments. It fosters even greater levels of commitment and productivity across the organization.

**How does the leader engage the organization?**
Engaging the organization through the methods cited above is no easy task. It requires persistence and determination. And when you add the use of culture as a context for organizational transformation, which alone occupies an entire section in this book, the task becomes even more daunting. But there is certain knowledge and a series of characteristics that can help the leader successfully move through this process.

First, know the organization. It is not sufficient to spout cursory information and statistics, you must present how these descriptors serve as a baseline for actions, the strategies required to execute them, and how the outcomes support future endeavors.

Next, engage individuals and groups to educate them on

your vision for the organization and to actively seek input. Apply the values and beliefs of the organization to promote change.

Also, know that you are the face of the organization—both inside and outside. Use this to your advantage to promote the vision and values, and help the community understand and support the organization.

Be aggressive in seeking professional development for your associates and yourself. It keeps all of you abreast of trends and best practices, enabling your colleagues to perform better in current roles while being prepared for future job opportunities.

Accept the responsibility to drive change. You will have critics due to the tough decisions you will have to make to do the right thing and focus on the future or make the organization healthy. Accept accountability when things go wrong and learn how to move forward. When you escape from a fire, you do not want to always smell like smoke. In other words, during difficult moments, figure out the most reasonable solution to benefit the organization so that the challenge does not drag on beyond its life.

A degree of fortitude is required to engage the organization as well—especially when change is required. This type of fortitude is not just the capacity to endure personal adversity, but also the ability to be purposeful and tenacious in inspiring people to move the organization forward.

Underlying this book's Three Essentials of Leadership—education, experience and exposure—is a systematic approach to help leaders engage the organization. Conveying a vision of the future organization is an important first step in the system, along with understanding how timing helps you identify internal and external opportunities that can help advance the vision and make provisions for the strategies and tactics needed to accomplish it. Benchmarks help measure the effectiveness of tactics and serve as a foundation for continual improvement. UnCLE, the Uninterrupted Cycle of Leadership Effectiveness, demonstrates the connection between these four components.

As you practice and hone your leadership skills, keep in mind you cannot carry out this responsibility alone. You must engage individuals and groups from throughout the organization by demonstrating your commitment to the growth of the organization and the individuals who will get the work done. This requires you to know the organization, be aggressive in driving change, and to exhibit fortitude.

# Culture as a Context for Organizational Transformation

Strategic priorities and the tactics required to achieve them must be developed in concert with constituencies from throughout your organization. This process ensures buy-in and execution at all levels. It facilitates the identification of cultural attributes of the organization, builds upon them, and then applies the results to foster employee involvement and the creation of a more open and responsive organization. Assessment and management of the culture is therefore pivotal to any organization's success.

Harvard University professor James L. Heskett says a strong corporate culture can account for 20 to 30 percent of the differential in corporate performance when compared with "culturally unremarkable" competitors. Edgar Schein, in his 1986 book *Organizational Culture and Leadership*, further suggests that organizational culture is the strongest influencer of leader and organizational effectiveness because of the following factors:

*...the most successful leaders pay attention to culture early in their tenure to uncover key attributes—both good and bad—that may affect attainment of goals and objectives*

- It is the operating system of an organization and derives its actions and guides how its members feel, think, and act.
- Culture encompasses the invisible beliefs, values, and assumptions of an organization.

- Productivity is directly influenced by the culture of an organization.
- The beliefs of the members are the strongest influence on an organization's culture.

My good friend and noted higher education leader, Christine McPhail, believes that the extent to which leaders benefit from these factors depends upon how well they correctly assess the culture and use the assessments to facilitate change through policies, strategies, and programs that are aligned with the organization's values and beliefs. The challenge, then, is transforming our notions of culture as a construct into operations that help achieve organizational goals.

That said, the most successful leaders pay attention to culture early in their tenure to uncover key attributes—both good and bad—that may affect attainment of goals and objectives. Maintaining a healthy culture requires constant attention—the CEO must have an active role in both its shaping
and development.

The Cultural Due Diligence Integrative Change Process (CDDICP), illustrated in the following diagram and introduced to me by Pittsburgh consultant Harold Shields, is illustrative of the process of transforming organizations with culture as a context. A cultural assessment is the initial step in the process, followed by the various independent stages that often overlap.

## Cultural Due Diligence Integrative Change Process

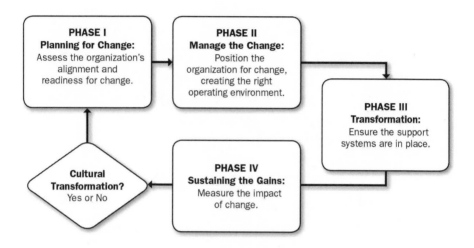

The information gathered from the cultural assessment in concert with the CDDICP makes it possible to recognize where the organization is now, so goals can be set for where the organization wants to be. Furthermore, the assessment brings to light those areas of the existing culture requiring help or modification to achieve the organization's stated purposes.

Once completed, the assessment serves as an indispensable tool for understanding and meeting the needs of the organization, its employees, and its customers. Performing a cultural assessment is an involved procedure, but surely worth the effort. The entire process requires considerable planning and preparation. The outcomes of cultural assessment promote cultural change systematically, but periodic re-assessment as depicted in the CDDICP ensures that practices are aligned with the organization's cultural values and beliefs over time.

**Cultural due diligence following a natural disaster**
I learned to trust and apply the outcomes of cultural
assessment during my chancellorship at Delgado
Community College in New Orleans, Louisiana, following
Hurricane Katrina, which landed on the Gulf Coast and
flooded virtually all of New Orleans beginning on August
29, 2005. Nearly 3,000 deaths were recorded and 644,500
residents were displaced. Individuals and organizations from
throughout America aided in the recovery. Following is just
a glimpse of the outpouring of support just several months
following the storm:

- 233,760 relief workers helped with the recovery
- $2.12 billion was raised
- 1,196 shelters were created to house 1.2 million families
  and 3.7 million individuals
- 348,000 instances of volunteerism occurred, nearly
  one-half of which (153,000) involved college students

One example of student volunteerism is the group from
Marietta College who traveled to Delgado to remove debris
and clean buildings. In another instance, students from
Centenary College sheltered, fed, and clothed 250 students
from Dillard University in New Orleans. Students from the
University of South Carolina traveled to Biloxi, Mississippi
to clean out homes, load and unload supplies, and distribute
meals. And students from Bentley College traveled to
southern Alabama to rebuild and improve the Bayou La
Batre Rural Health Clinic.

Because of the storm, 20 of Delgado's 25 buildings were
damaged or destroyed. Nearly all 17,500 students and many
of the faculty and staff were displaced, and classes were
canceled until January 2006.

But faculty and staff, whose personal losses included the
destruction of their homes, the scattering of family, and the

deaths of friends and acquaintances, banded together to prepare the campus for the return of students. Volunteers sat under an awning in the parking lot at the college's City Park Campus during an unusually frigid December to distribute information on how to register for the upcoming spring 2006 semester.

In every area of the college's operations, people had to invent and implement new ways to accomplish ordinary, day-to-day tasks. I imagined such resiliency and dedication was a cultural asset that served the college steadfastly, perhaps even before Hurricane Katrina. But I wanted to test this assumption. If authenticated, the results could serve to develop a roadmap for the recovery of Delgado.

When searching for a tool, Harold Shields introduced me to the little known, but highly effective, Culture's Contextual Elements (CCE) questionnaire, which provides a clear picture of the extent to which certain characteristics shape the culture of an organization. The CCE quantifies the impact of culture on commitment and productivity, allows for the study of other factors deemed important to the organization's development, and assists in identifying actions that contribute systematically to the excellence necessary to become a more self-regarding institution.

The CCE asks respondents to rate 25 culturally relevant items on a five-point scale from "Severe" to "Excellent" in the areas of involvement, accountability, adaptability, and communication: all useful in assessing organizational behavior and the culture that embodies it.

## Culture Contextual Elements Rating Scales

| | | |
|---|---|---|
| Severe | issue in the culture that must be addressed immediately. | 1.00 -1.80 (60.0 percent – 68.0 percent) |
| Symptomatic | of a troubled culture that must be addressed soon or could become severe. | 1.81 - 2.60 (68.1 percent – 76.0 percent) |
| Significant | to improvement of culture and must be monitored and addressed in the near future. | 2.61- 3.40 (76.1 percent – 84.0 percent) |
| Positive | indication that the culture is supporting the mission, vision and values of the organization. | 3.41 - 4.20 (84.1 percent – 92.0 percent) |
| Excellent | cultural element to be built upon and conveyed as strength of the organization. | 4.21 – 5.00 (92.1 percent – 100 percent) |

The first CCE component, involvement, can serve to promote a culture of teamwork and collaboration. This requires greater knowledge and understanding of the goals of the organization, as well as recognizing how individuals can contribute to achieving them through their collective work and individual roles and responsibility. In this area, the CCE measures the extent that individuals are fully developed and empowered with authority, initiative, and ability.

The second area, consistency, is important for creating a culture of transparency that requires candor and trust at every level of the organization. It is established through open dialogue, a commitment to policies and practices that are congruent, and support and recognition for calculated risk-taking. Along these lines, the CCE seeks to determine if, based on shared values and beliefs, clear expectations are set and adhered to at every step along the way.

Next, adaptability means a culture of openness and flexibility where the workplace accommodates employee transformation and the needs of external stakeholders. In this area, the CCE calculates the degree to which the culture can readily accommodate anticipated and unexpected change.

And finally, communication entails understanding the organization's progress against strategic priorities to create a culture committed to open dialogue. Regularly communicating the vision of the organization, updating key constituencies on the status and outcomes of initiatives, and seeking input are ways that open communication is enhanced. The CCE measures the extent to which the vision, direction, and status of the organization are clearly understood and embraced by others.

With respect to the CCE results for Delgado Community College, scores for each cultural element and overall ranged from 2.85 to 3.67 (78.5 to 89.7 percent), with an overall score of 3.26 (83.3 percent). The scores and percentages for each of the cultural elements are summarized in the following chart:

| CCE Category | Score | Percentage |
|---|---|---|
| Involvement | 3.40 | 83.4 percent |
| Consistency | 2.85 | 72.9 percent |
| Adaptability | 3.10 | 78.5 percent |
| Communication | 3.67 | 83.1 percent |
| OVERALL | 3.26 | 83.3 percent |

These outcomes were an indication that the college had a solid cultural foundation of teamwork and collaboration to aid in its recovery from Hurricane Katrina and build for the future. Among the recommendations for achieving this aim were:

- Continue to encourage and reward creativity. Build a culture that allows for risk-taking to improve productivity, efficiency in work processes, and teamwork. Feedback, both positive and critical, can strengthen institutional processes and, when accepted, can improve enthusiasm.
- Institute regular, timely notification of policies and procedures, detailing how they promote sound decision-making, enable clear expectations for involvement in addressing critical issues, and set forth standards for personnel actions.
- Create a flexible, strategic direction for the organization. This will allow challenges to productivity and change to be addressed by the college. While the structure, policies, and procedures must be evident, individuals in decision- making roles must be held accountable for applying them in an efficient and productive manner.

- Expand communication processes to accommodate individuals at all levels. This will increase the knowledge and understanding of the college's direction and increase comfort levels in responding to various initiatives.

In surveying my colleagues at Delgado, what I expected to find held true. Their values and beliefs, in association with a culture of collaboration, were evident before the storm and heightened by their commitment to a larger effort called "Come Home to Delgado." Some of the faculty and staff resided in temporary housing placed on the campus by FEMA, the Federal Emergency Management Agency. By reopening the school for returning students, they derived personal and professional satisfaction that positively affected the college's culture.

The recovery effort began with the evacuation from New Orleans on August 27, 2005, two days before Hurricane Katrina struck the Gulf Coast. Daphne and I traveled to Atlanta, to the home of my sister, Angela. Upon the realization that the storm had exacted significant damage to the city and college, Daphne went on to Youngstown, Ohio, to reside with her sister, Doshia. She would not return to New Orleans until almost three months later.

I headed for Baton Rouge to set up a temporary headquarters on the campus of Baton Rouge Community College. Those members of the administrative team that did assemble at the headquarters constituted a small, but mighty, team. We began the arduous tasks associated with reopening the college.

The former emergency response plan was ineffective for dealing with this significant natural disaster, so we had to formulate a new plan. Our intent was to reopen the college no later than the 2006 spring semester. To accomplish this, we prioritized the following measures:

- Develop an emergency website to enable students to contact us and, if possible, continue their education physically or online at colleges in the communities where they evacuated.
- Expand communications through the website and other means to locate and update staff and faculty on the status of the recovery.
- Recover and reboot information technology hardware and systems located at the redundant site in downtown New Orleans.
- Cultivate relationships with government officials to secure support and funding.
- Remediate and open buildings (as possible) to hold classes; mainly on the City Park Campus located in western New Orleans.
- Establish temporary housing for faculty and staff, placed on the campus by FEMA.

These actions were separate and apart from our "Come Home to Delgado" campaign, which concluded with classes being reinstated January 2006, with an enrollment of 10,002. Despite this nearly miraculous recovery, looking back a few months later, we identified several mechanisms to improve the emergency response plan in place before the storm:

- Identify the emergency leadership team early and include officials responsible for curriculum, finance, human resources, information technology, marketing and communications, facilities and government regulations, and compliance.

- Provide this team with laptops that have wireless capability, cell phones that can also serve as pagers, hotspots, and satellite phones. Also, make certain the telephone numbers have area codes outside of the affected area.
- Select—in advance—a headquarters where the team can temporarily gather following the emergency.
- Develop a well-established communications protocol that includes a website which allows updates and provides access to information on college operations.
- Secure a back-up site for information technology that is well outside the range of flood grounds. Most organizations are now going to cloud-based systems for this purpose.
- Ensure emergency management and government officials have access to buildings.
- Given the variety and extent of the interpersonal challenges experienced by faculty, staff, and students, provide counseling services in person and on-line to those who need it.

As I reflect on the impact the storm and its recovery had on my leadership development, several things come to mind. First, during a crisis you must set aside—to the degree you can—personal concerns. The roof and windows of my home in the New Orleans' west bank community of English Turn were damaged by strong winds and rain.

My primary focus, however, was on getting the institution reopened with the involvement of my colleagues, many of whom completely lost their homes in the disaster.

In responding to Hurricane Katrina, and by implication other crises, every action was and should be launched individually and each subsequent action built upon the preceding one. There was no recourse except a day-by-day response to the disruption caused by Hurricane Katrina. This environment required me to make difficult choices. Due to a state budget shortfall and requirements to balance the budget, I released one-third of Delgado's workforce, especially those unable to return to their roles due to the storm-related personal issues.

As I explained earlier, some members of the executive staff were not able to immediately join me at the emergency headquarters. In fact, most of my colleagues who arrived did not necessarily represent senior leadership, but rather a cross-section of the college community who understood the importance of collective effort to expedite the recovery. They were motivated, enthusiastic, and willing to learn and apply techniques outside of their comfort zone. They recommended and led activities to aid reopening the college, on occasion working 12-hour days to complete their tasks. This proves, in part, the importance of hiring capable and dedicated individuals who remain committed to the organization during times of challenge.

The actions of this small band of comrades enabled me to be focused sharply on representing the vision and strategy for the recovery. I was the president who sat with them daily as we planned; who was by their sides as these plans were executed; and who represented them proudly with government officials and philanthropists as I searched for resources to aid the school's reopening.

**Joseph C. Canizaro, Columbus Properties**
Among the stalwart supporters of Delgado and New Orleans

is businessman Joseph C. Canizaro, who arguably is among the most astute business leaders in America. Like other residents, Hurricane Katrina damaged his new home located west of the city. And like other residents, he set aside his home's reconstruction to assist with the monumental task of rebuilding New Orleans as a member of Mayor Ray Nagin's 17-member rebuilding commission, which issued a blueprint for the city's revival.

Canizaro believed Delgado could be beneficial in restoring New Orleans' historic buildings based on techniques applied in the United Kingdom through the Built Environment program of the Prince Charles Foundation. So, during the recovery efforts, and with the support of Canizaro, I traveled with my colleagues to London, England to determine how techniques developed there could be taught at Delgado and applied to rebuild New Orleans.

According to Bonnie Warren in her article "50 Years of Faith and Vision," Canizaro's hard-charging style infuriated some community leaders when he suggested some of the city's lowest-lying neighborhoods—mostly occupied by prior and black residents—may need to be forsaken. His suggestion never took hold, but the areas he referenced are taking the longest to recover mainly because their evacuees did not return to them or re-located to other communities in the city.

Canizaro credits his success to his late father, a surgeon in Biloxi, Mississippi, who modeled deliberateness. This characteristic allowed him to become an astute business analyst and to recognize and nurture talented individuals. His commitment to the rebuilding of New Orleans is symbolic of many individuals who worked tirelessly during the aftermath of Hurricane Katrina.

Like these individuals, members of the Delgado community would be prepared for what lay ahead with a renewed commitment to collaboration. Their training began following Hurricane Katrina as they gathered and united to reopen the college. A commitment to collective action was formed and from it emerged new leaders who were willing to take on responsibility. Some of these emerging leaders went on to earn doctoral degrees, and two are now campus chief executive officers.

For many years, experts on organizational development have recognized the power and influence of culture on operations and development. Culture is often represented in beliefs and values that must be converted into practical elements to be measured and strengthened as a means of improving organizational outcomes. This process ensures commitment, facilitates achieving desired outcomes, and helps validate your personalized approach to leadership.

Through the framework introduced in this section, provided by the CDDICP, assessment and management of culture is pivotal to the success of an organization. At the core of the CDDICP is an assessment instrument like the CCE questionnaire, which measures four distinct and tangible cultural operations—involvement, consistency, adaptability, and communication. This became my most useful tool.

# VII. Other Considerations in Refining Your Personalized Approach

*Additional attributes and abilities such as managing as leader, looking like a leader, recognizing and responding to challenges, honoring diversity and developing yourself and your colleagues for the future.*

In his article, "Evolution of the Manager," Jacob Morgan argues the constant debate around whether we need more managers or more leaders is a fruitless one that artificially pits the two against each other. When thinking about the future of work, leaders must be managers in moving the organization forward based on the nature of the enterprise and its strategic priorities. In the first several pages that follow, I present examples from my leadership roles and those of others to illustrate how the leader carries out this important responsibility.

Sir Richard Branson is among the most successful businessmen in the world. One of his leadership principles is the importance of being visible. A visible leader, Branson believes, is all about carefully crafting image—without being dishonest. Image is how you look, but it's also who you are. Following this section, in showing you tasks and encounters you will most likely face and for which you must be prepared, I offer a glimpse of how leadership should look.

In the next section, among the more important in the book, I explore the challenges of leadership to provide a broader description of the various circumstances you will need to avoid. Incoherent and inconsistent vision and strategy are among the elements that can derail your leadership opportunity.

Many of these issues can be overcome. Graham Jones, author of "Avoiding the Perils of the Accidental Leader," believes leaders must possess a resilient self-belief and maintain motivation when things are tough. They must be able to remain in control when the pressure is at its fiercest, allowing them to bounce back from setbacks.

Finally, I offer a view of the importance of an inclusive organization and your role in creating an environment that welcomes individuals with diverse perspectives and exceptional skill sets. This discussion leads to the final section of this chapter, where I offer a view of leadership as it might evolve. This is an important chance to gain insight on how your approach can be modified and improved for the future.

# Leader as a Manager to Attain Organizational Excellence Through UnCLE

Your personalized leadership approach is the product of the Three Essentials of Leadership—education, experience, and exposure—and the establishment of special skills, competencies, and processes described throughout *Change the Lapel Pin*. So now you either have been—or are about to be—elected to a leadership role, in part because you are educated, experienced, and imbued with the characteristics of leaders you admire.

Over the past few years, you have been a successful manager of strategies and operations and, more importantly, a respected and able colleague. Now it is time to take those characteristics with you as you move onward and upward. You do not leave them behind as you transition to a formal leadership role. It could be implied, then, that you were a leader as a manager. You just have not been exposed to the trappings that come with the leadership role: the formal title; extensive executive-level responsibilities; and technical requirements, such as creating vision and strategies and representing the organization's interest to the public. As you transition to your leadership responsibilities, the skills you developed and adroitly applied as a manager will be necessary.

In fact, they will be important from day one as you learn the organization and its people.

Here is how I applied both leader and management principles in my presidency at Cuyahoga based on UnCLE, which was introduced in a previous chapter. Remember, UnCLE is what allows you to respond to causes, for example trends and predicaments that might be disruptive to your organization. Next, UnCLE helps in identifying the short and long-term solutions to address the cause. Then, UnCLE asks you to measure the outcomes of the solutions. And finally, UnCLE allows you to celebrate and build upon these outcomes or introduce another cause. Hopefully, through this example, you can apply a similar process to your own leadership role.

**UnCLE Step 1: Identify a cause for action**
Start by asking the following questions:

- What are the trends that will disrupt your business?
- What impact will they have on your organization?
- What do the data indicate?
- How should we respond?

My current presidency at Cuyahoga Community College arrived at a challenging time in our nation's history. At that moment, the educational attainment of Americans aged 25 to 34 years old was ranked 16th among developing countries; Ohio placed 39th among the 50 states in degree attainment. In Cleveland, the skills gap meant only about 67 percent of available workers could compete for more high-wage, high-tech jobs. And the college's student attainment was unsatisfactory for an institution of our size and stature. This environment became our cause for action in accordance with step one of UnCLE.

As the president, I recognized immediately that I would have to respond to this new form of "a nation at risk" to get individuals the degrees and certificates they sought in a timely manner and then guide them toward meaningful careers or four-year institutions.

**UnCLE Step 2: Identify the strategies and tactics to address the cause for action**
Next, identify:

- What are the short and long-term strategies to address the cause for action?
- Do they reflect national best practices and innovations developed and applied at your organization?
- Are they actionable and measurable?

The UnCLE model requires organizations to establish mechanisms that respond to a cause—something that would address an important matter, rally the organization around it, and set out the steps to address it. The focus on improving educational attainment required us to essentially transform the college by identifying overall priorities, reframing the college, and implementing specific campus-based and college-wide actions.

**College priorities**
Our response as an institution was to improve the rate and number by which students earn certificates and degrees. The term "Success and Completion," found in the center of the following chart, is the primary goal to be attained through the six priorities I introduced earlier in the book and further expand upon here. They are also found on this chart:

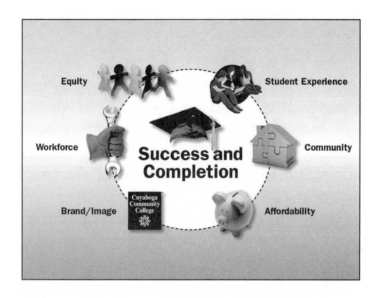

**Student Experience.** First, it was our desire to provide students with a more holistic experience outside the classroom. Such an experience was aimed at increasing their involvement with the college through amenities such as: workspaces that feature innovative technology; programs and activities that connected them with their peers; athletics and other events as participants and spectators; and attractive and modern facilities.

**Community.** We built upon Cuyahoga's strong legacy of collaboration and engagement with our community. That connection was nurtured as we sought to increase partnerships with educational, business, government, and non-profit institutions for the benefit of our students. We established that we needed to work with our K-12 school partners to ensure that students, regardless of their ethnic or economic backgrounds, were prepared for college coursework and could complete a certificate or degree in a prescribed timeframe.

**Affordability.** We sought to re-prioritize our resources to improve student achievement. Tuition was held constant for students with increased course loads and higher grade point averages. Textbook costs were reduced through collaboration with the bookstore contractor and free or reduced-cost online educational resources were identified. All students received a free public transportation pass.

These savings for students were especially important to reducing their time to graduation. They were also benefitting the college through Ohio's funding model, which is based entirely on students' ability to complete coursework and finish degrees and certificates. So, it was imperative that Cuyahoga enrolled more students and decreased the time it took them to graduate, especially to secure additional state monies.

The state allocation is combined with monies from tuition and fees and funding from two county tax levies, placed on the ballot every five years, to comprise the college's three fundamental revenue streams. Forty-four percent of the college's annual operating budget comes from the levies, so the marketing campaigns to secure their passage are extensive and require widespread participation by the college community and external partners, who help raise significant private dollars for operations, materials (including signage), and media exposure.

**Brand/Image.** As the landscape of information is changing rapidly in the greater Cleveland area and around the world, we also needed to present the college in effective and innovative ways. We knew we had to convey, loudly and clearly, the stories of our successes to outside audiences and, through internal communications, keep the college community updated on priorities and actions they helped create.

**Workforce.** We were required to work more closely with employers to ensure that we were supplying their current and future employees with certificates and degrees with labor market value—all fortified by liberal arts courses that make them well-rounded as workers and informed and productive as citizens.

**Equity.** And finally, we applied the concept "inclusive excellence," championed by the Association of American Colleges and Universities (AAC&U) as a mechanism for ensuring everyone understood their role in helping minority students excel at the same or higher rates as all students. This meant programs and services for students were integrated and specific organizations, like the Black American Council and the Hispanic Council, would work individually with incoming and first-generation students, especially to provide mentoring and other supports to improve their chances of obtaining a degree or certificate. I provide a more detailed discussion on equity in an upcoming section on diversity and inclusion in the workforce.

### Reframing the college
These six strategic priorities required me to be intimately involved as a manager in developing and implementing the actions to meet these lofty and ambitious goals. This is the area where leadership and management combine. I surmised

that rather than a "top down, bottom up" philosophy to organizational development, my ambitions required that collaborations, decisions, and work be carried out on middle ground.

To accommodate the approach, I had to flatten a particularly hierarchical organizational structure to reflect one that ensured greater connection and communication at a micro-level. A form of "matrix management" is also evident at the college, which means some programs are operated by individuals who only have a "dotted" or indirect reporting line to the administrator at the program site. This non-supervisory arrangement requires productive relationships between the parties to work effectively.

In addition to a less vertical organizational framework, I had to improve our ability to function interpersonally within the matrix structure as well. This is where the Culture's Contextual Elements (CCE) questionnaire and the Cultural Due Diligence Integrative Change Process (CDDICP), described in the previous section, were instrumental.

After administering the CCE during the summer of 2013, the overall score of 2.99, or 79.9 percent, indicated certain aspects of the culture could be strengthened by creating an environment where heightened teamwork and collaboration in response to strategic priorities was the norm.

The details on the following page represent the recommendations we received from our consultant who administered the CCE and interpreted the results.

Recommendations:
- Ensure employees are challenged and empowered to carry out the operations of the college by providing ample professional development to establish skills and

competencies for current and future organizational changes and initiatives.

- Continue to build processes to gain consensus around critical issues.
- Promote ways where employees can more readily adapt to change.
- Convey through communications and publications a consistent and understandable image of the college.

To develop responses to these recommendations, four teams were created from the College-Wide Cabinet, comprised of administrators from across the college. They gathered each month to discuss proposed actions, suggest how they might be implemented, and prepare to report to the College-Wide Cabinet on the outcomes of their deliberations.

The recommendations of the four teams were implemented broadly and, as a result, specific cultural elements of the CCE were improved to the extent that the Fall 2016 results showed an overall score of 3.56, or 85.6 percent. This was a 0.51, or 5.7 percent, improvement from the first administration of the CCE in 2013.

Restructuring the college and strengthening its culture were important first steps of the middle ground approach implemented in response to the six strategic priorities. More important, however, was ensuring that college groups understood their roles in making certain the college programs addressed the pressing educational needs in the greater Cleveland area and beyond. The College-Wide Cabinet was certainly at the forefront of this effort. But at the root of the middle ground was the President's Council, comprised of faculty leaders from bargaining and academic groups and chief administrative officers. This group evaluates the effectiveness of current approaches in response to our six strategic priorities and considers others that can be piloted or scaled. Recommendations are then implemented and evaluated at each of the four campuses.

**Specific campus-based initiatives**
Success Centers were established at local high schools to prepare students for the college experience. As they arrived, the First-Year Experience (FYE) program, featuring two semester-long student success courses and other intentional and mandatory activities, provided students with a more structured start to college.

Efforts to improve grades in English and mathematics helped students remain on a more dependable "guided pathway" to earning a degree. And a paid internship experience at a college or business location kept students connected to the college during the summer months.

Accentuating these efforts at each campus are Care Teams that provide individualized attention to students, tracked using specially designed technology called One Record. A research and development component, the One Door, was the mechanism for gathering individuals from throughout the college to explore and study best practices developed at Cuyahoga and beyond that might add value to the existing efforts.

**College-wide actions**
Undergirding these student-facing activities were the administrative units of the college. "SMART" (Specific, Measurable, Agreed-Upon, Realistic, and Time-Based) goals now populated an evaluation system that recognized

and rewarded individual and collective contributions to student success. Scholarships, tuition incentives, textbook affordability, public transportation passes, and other efficiency measures keep costs for students low. Technology, including social media, improved connections to the college from jobs and homes. And vastly expanded and viable short-term training programs got individuals into quality jobs sooner.

## UnCLE Step III: Measure success against internal expectations and external norms and standards and build upon the outcomes

Again, this process requires asking yourself several questions:

- How do we measure success of the strategies and tactics?
- Do the outcomes support them?
- Can we celebrate and build upon the results to improve organizational capacity?
- What do the outcomes suggest in determining next steps?

Fifty-one performance measures were identified to measure the effectiveness of responses to our six strategic priorities. For example, according to several benchmarks beginning with the baseline year of 2010 and ending in 2017, we witnessed increases of nearly 100 percent in graduates completing degrees and certificates and a 400 percent increase in the rate at which they completed these credentials.

The charts on the following page illustrate these important outcomes.

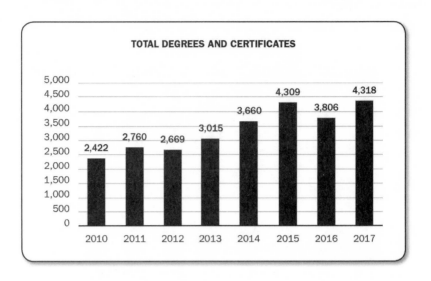

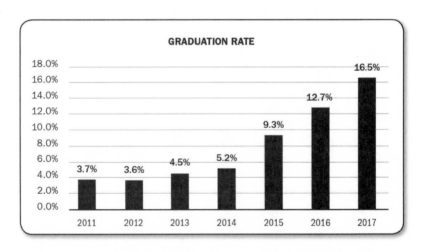

According to the magazine, *Community College Times,* these accomplishments place our institution among the top of the nation's 1108 community colleges. At the same time, students continued their education at increased levels and exhibited improved success in mathematics and English courses that serve as so-called "gateways" to degrees and certificates.

In recognition of these achievements and the college's overarching success, Cuyahoga received the prestigious Bellwether Award from the Community College Futures Assembly for achievements in workforce development programming. The Kisko Foundation recognized the college's commitment to veterans and their families with the Kohlberg Prize, which included a cash award to offset the cost of a new veteran's center at the Western Campus.

For the first time in its decade-long association with Achieving the Dream, whose goal is to improve educational outcomes for minority students, Cuyahoga qualified for the organization's prestigious Leah Meyer Austin Award. And through its Commission on Economic Inclusion, the Greater Cleveland Partnership (the economic development organization of the city) recognized the college for a third time as "Best in Class" for its commitment to a diverse workforce.

This was a moment to celebrate the college's achievements and to think about how we could use the current momentum to take the college to even greater heights.

## UnCLE Step IV: Introduce the next wave of organizational refinements and innovations

In the final step, these are the questions you must ask to pull everything together:

- Is our approach productive?
- Can we implement and sustain the outcomes?
- What is the next iteration of our response to the current or emerging sense of urgency?

Our intent moving forward is to increase commitment to our six strategic priorities and intensify efforts to graduate more students of color, students who are economically disadvantaged, and students who enroll after joining the workforce. We also aim to increase access to the college by high school students through the state's dual enrollment program, College Credit Plus, which allows students in seventh grade and beyond to enroll in college level courses. In 2017, the college graduated 28 students who earned degrees and high school diplomas simultaneously.

Internally, we will be identifying and eliminating barriers in the students' experience that interfere with their education. And we will introduce more workforce short-term certificate programs to add to an already expanded array of offerings. These programs require new equipment and modernized or updated facilities.

## The mixture of manager and leader

As you can see, leaders do not always operate from a lofty position. In considering the UnCLE process, it can also be implied the business of organizational development requires the leader to operate as a manager.

Leadership experts see this melding of the manager and leader as vital. Jacob Morgan of the Future Organization believes the transition between manager and leader is not abrupt—it is ongoing. Great managers can also become great leaders as they make the transition. They earn leadership through their ability to foster productivity by supporting and advocating for their employees. This carries over as they mature and grow. The basis of their efforts is dependent upon collective engagement and thought. Their management styles include leading by example and a general willingness to carry out—or at least greatly understand—the work performed by others.

There are few boundaries set for work processes. Evaluations are made in real-time and provide a mechanism for feedback that praises the efforts of employees or describes how performance can be readily improved.

In this context, however, you must not micromanage. Yet, just as in situational leadership, you should identify the appropriate level of engagement necessary based on each individual situation and the readiness level of the employee and organization.

A great time to apply this principle is at the very beginning of any leadership role. As time progresses, and the organization makes strides toward improvement, it may be smart to withdraw from direct engagement and concentrate on those matters where your ongoing involvement is expected. As a college president, for example, these may include matters of the Board of Trustees, fundraising, government affairs, civic outreach, and special projects—like research and development.

# Images of Leadership:
# How Does It Look and Feel?

Models of leadership are powerful in helping you formulate your personalized approach. They serve as examples of how to respond to certain conditions when your skill set is limited or you want to refine your competence in specific instances and areas. The iconic leaders introduced in this section also remind you that your leadership fabric, the items that constitute your style, is more than just talent, education, and experience. Woven into this fabric, too, are the threads of your personal encounters, whether conscious or subliminal, good or bad.

These individuals not only exhibit exemplary leadership qualities, but make you feel inspired by their presence. This sentiment is expressed by noted author Maya Angelou, who said, "At the end of the day, people won't remember what you said or did, they will remember how you made them feel."

In his article "What Does Leadership Feel Like," Kevin Berchelman makes the following conclusion:

> *"Good leaders get our discretionary effort because we appreciate how they make us feel—about them, about ourselves and about the organization. They have integrity you can feel, knowing in your heart that they're going to do what they say—or own up to it when they can't. Because of that, you trust them. They are genuine, comfortable with who they are. You are certain of what they stand for and what they care about without them saying so. They are attentive and, consequently, make you feel like a conversation with them is important. They are not distracted by what else is important to them. It is very calming."*

The imagery and emotional impact provided by individuals you respect is not inconsequential. They will benefit you as you grow and develop in your work. The examples that follow are not exhaustive, but illustrate how you might identify and model certain leadership behaviors.

## Internal operations

Hindsight is a powerful thing. When we can assess something that has already happened and look back, it gives us new perspective. It makes us ask, "Why did I encounter this person? Why did I not see the truth of this situation? What am I supposed to learn from this incident?"

Never have I felt the impulse to ask these questions more than when my late friend, Dr. Robert Callaway, died at age 45. He and I met at Winston-Salem State University. We cemented our friendship over pickup basketball games at lunchtime, discussing, among other things, careers in higher education.

Robert looked to me as a mentor. He was always searching for ways he could improve himself by observing individuals he aspired to be like. People who really pulled themselves up by their bootstraps, who have made their way in the world and have taken advantage of every opportunity they could—those are the people that appealed to him.

Robert saw me as one of these people. He admired that I overcame humble beginnings to attain leadership roles at institutions of higher learning. Like me, he became a community college zealot, almost fanatical in his commitment and belief in the egalitarian institutions. These institutions satisfied his personal convictions and professional aspirations, which included one day becoming a college president. I encouraged him to earn his doctorate and use it as a springboard for that advancement.

And he did earn his PhD at Bowling Green State University. Afterwards, he secured a position at Lorain County Community College (LCCC) ultimately becoming the division dean of Social Sciences and Human Services. Our face-to-face conversations grew fewer, but we kept in touch by phone and email.

Robert's career was well on its way. The next position for him probably would have been a vice presidency, followed by a presidency, but unfortunately, he didn't get that far. Just two weeks before he died on January 9, 2009, Robert left me a holiday greeting on my voicemail. I was unable to respond immediately, and that inaction haunts me still.

LCCC President Dr. Roy Church tagged me as Robert's mentor in his introduction of me before I gave reflections at the crowded funeral service. And while I appreciated Dr. Church's reference, I realize now I learned more from Robert than he gained from me. I am embarrassed to confess I originally saw Robert only as a jock. He even "walked and talked" like an athlete; a basketball player whose team I always wanted to be on.

Robert was a winner. He had great skills. His head was always in the game. On the basketball court he guided us, taught us how to get open for the lay-up, and praised us when we made the shot. But because of our mentor and protégé relationship, I was incapable of acknowledging his superior court skills were anything but leadership attributes.

Robert's penchant for hard work, his competitive nature, and his tenacity were among his considerable talents—gifts honed through his interactions with family, neighbors, and friends on the blacktop courts in Newark, New Jersey.

The point guard in basketball (Robert's position) is one of the purest instances of leadership in a team-oriented environment. It is unlike football or baseball, where leadership depends on whether the team is on offense or defense. In football, the quarterback is the leader on offense and the middle linebacker is the leader on defense. In baseball, when the team is on the field, it is the catcher who signals possible throws for consideration by the pitcher. And when batting, the coaching staff prepares the batter for the types of pitches that might be thrown. But in basketball, it is the point guard who is responsible for directing the team regardless of the circumstances.

In his capacity as point guard, Robert had to learn the "playbook" through education and training provided by the head coach. He applied the skills he honed in practices during games, where his actions looked instinctual. I am confident that during practices he experimented with being spontaneous in preparation of the inevitable breakdown of a play during the game.

He probably also examined videotape to prepare for the opposing team and to understand how his actions on the court fostered the success of the team. Perhaps he studied the attributes of other point guards to emulate some of their characteristics he felt would benefit his play. Robert idolized point guard legends Earvin "Magic" Johnson of the Los Angeles Lakers and Isaiah Thomas of the Detroit Pistons. As the point guard, Robert had to represent the culture of the team. He had to exemplify a culture of fortitude, particularly when the team was not performing optimally.

It might appear I have overly-exaggerated the basketball analogy. But it is true that point guard play can be an example of how leaders conduct their responsibilities. Point guards on the court and leaders in organizations need to learn principles that qualify them for their roles. Leaders are required to create a playbook—a strategic plan—that guides their approach to advancing the organization. Like point guards, leaders might seek examples from other professionals to expand their skill set. And leaders must promote the cultural elements of the organization that contribute to its success. Point guards must accentuate the culture as well and, like leaders, be prepared for any eventuality when excerpts from the playbook do not work.

To me, Robert was exactly what leadership looks like.

### External matters

In connection with Robert's death, I formed the belief that the people with whom you relate, on top of knowledge and experience, can have an important impact on who you are and the type of leader you could possibly become.

Robert's example, through his basketball playing and professional contributions, is plainly what leadership looks like to me on a day-to-day basis. There are other times, though, when leaders must traverse external environments that require a unique skill set.

For example, networking is a duty that can result in connections which promote better understanding of the organization. A leader who best exemplifies this quality was my predecessor at Cuyahoga, Jerry Sue Thornton, who was and continues to be, a sought-after advisor; distinguished for her contributions to almost every effort during her tenure to educationally strengthen the nation, the state of Ohio and the greater Cleveland area. In retirement, she still contributes to various community initiatives and is staunchly committed to helping two-year colleges and their presidents succeed.

She was astute at networking and political engagement that promoted and enriched Cuyahoga's brand, and she brought resources to the college for innovative programs and facilities. One example is the Corporate College, whose mission has been to provide highly specialized education at corporations, in some instances, throughout the country. Centers of Excellence were established as specially-designed, instructional delivery systems allowing students to develop competencies and skills or earn certificates and degrees that lead immediately to high-tech, high-wage jobs.

A highly acclaimed jazz studies program was created featuring JazzFest, which now attracts an audience of more than 30,000 spectators annually. She established the Presidential Scholarship Luncheon in 1992 to bring in renowned speakers, including President William "Bill" Clinton and George W. Bush, who, as of the 25th Anniversary of the event, helped raise scholarship funds totaling $18.5 million.

Thornton's legacy is not only an uncompromising commitment to students, but to one of the most well-appointed colleges in the nation. A college that includes such physical amenities as the Gill and Tommy LiPuma Center for Creative Arts, the KeyBank Public Safety Center, and the Medical Mutual Health Careers Center.

### Words matter
Networking provides a chance to convey to everyone the status of the organization, so the ability to impart a quality message is another important skill leaders need. The information should be concise so that the points are easily remembered and shared. Too much information, and the listener suffers from overload. Too little, and you miss an opportunity to share your message.

Sandy Shugart is someone who has mastered the art of

quality messaging as president of Orlando's Valencia College; this according to Fawn Johnson in "Community College's Big Ideas are Transforming Education." Valencia is a large, urban college focused on serving more than 70,000 students a year and noted for receiving the first Aspen Prize for community college excellence, which included a cash award of one million dollars.

Shugart is a proponent of the national movement that challenges the traditional, romantic notions of college, noting that only 17 percent of college students go to school full-time, live on campus, or complete a four-year degree at one institution. He points out that community colleges cater to the mundane parts of the college experience. Their aim is to quickly and effectively give students the skills they need to get a job with a decent salary. Community colleges train people for stable careers in accounting, electronics, nursing, and information technology.

Noted for his many platitudes that summarize this commitment, Shugart's most familiar adage—and No. 1 big idea—is that "anyone can learn anything under the right conditions." This means students' success is everyone's job and he places an emphasis on experimenting with new methods to see what's possible. Professional development is available to ensure this responsibility can be fulfilled. For example, full-time faculty members are required to complete a three-year learning academy in which they invent and test theories about how to improve student learning.

Shugart's second big idea, "start right," places a big emphasis on the "front door," ensuring students have success early and often in the 15 to 20 gateway courses that comprise 40 percent of the curriculum for first-year students.

Next is "connection and direction." All students are

expected to map out a graduation plan in their first semester. They must connect with faculty members, career advisers, tutors, and student-services staffers. Tutors, usually students themselves, know the professors and often sit in on classes to seek out students who might feel shy about asking for help. Tutoring centers are located in central campus areas, and they are packed.

Shugart's fourth big idea is "The college is how the students experience us, not how we experience them." This philosophy allows for the evaluation of what students need to experience compared to what they are experiencing. The environment is subsequently transformed to ensure that the total college environment contributes to learning and success.

Valencia constantly shares student achievement data focused on the instructor's actions to engage students: How has the instructor measured their own progress? Has she taken student outcomes seriously in her experiments with teaching methods? These are just a few of the elements associated with Shugart's fifth big idea, "The purpose of assessment is to improve learning."

"Collaboration" is the last big idea. It should come as little surprise that Shugart is a proponent of consensus, but he believes committees are time consuming. Instead, he is fond of calling 200 people into structured meetings. He then splits them into smaller groups that analyze specific questions. After a set amount of time, they reconvene as one large group, review the responses and break back up into smaller groups again to reach accord. It's a technique designed to quickly reach a strong set of actionable ideas that everyone buys into.

The value of Shugart's approach is that it serves as another example of how an important attribute I have already presented, communication, can serve as a flexible tool for obtaining input and building consensus on how to handle an organization's most-pressing responsibilities. It is also an example of how experienced leaders apply a technique long-term and consistently to build commitment and trust.

In selecting Valencia as the best community college in America, Aspen Institute officials noted that 51 percent of the college's full-time students graduate or transfer within three years of entering the school—a rate significantly higher than the national average of 39 percent. Valencia has experienced dramatic increases in graduation rates among college-ready African-American students as well, nearly tripling in the last decade from 15.4 percent to 44.3 percent. Graduation rates for college-ready Hispanic students have similarly impressive gains, jumping from 38.7 percent to 45.5 percent over the last decade.

### The power of presence

The image of leadership is often personified by a stalwart demeanor, especially during challenge and controversy. Among the leaders I personally know, the one who exudes this quality is Walter Bumphus, my former boss in Louisiana and current President of the American Association of Community Colleges (AACC). In this capacity at AACC, he commissioned a report in response to President Barack Obama's call in 2009 for a 50 percent increase in the number of college graduates by 2020. The result is *Reclaiming the American Dream: A Report from the 21st-Century Commission on the Future of Community Colleges*, which calls for dramatic changes to America's community colleges to ensure they contribute to this goal.

Bumphus' report centers on three areas of reform:

redesign, reinvent and reset. These are defined as a redesign of students' educational experiences, a reinvention of institutional roles, and a resetting of the system to create partnerships and incentives for student and institutional success. Nearly every community college in the nation uses the report to identify, develop, and assess their actions to improve student educational attainment.

In addition to his current role, Bumphus served as the head of the Louisiana Community and Technical College System. Under his leadership, the reputation of the statewide system grew because of its increased role in workforce training and development. But because of some state politicians who perceived Bumphus, a black man, as a threat to the status quo, he was often confronted during legislative hearings where he was attempting to bring additional resources to the institutions under his leadership.

On one such occasion, a rural state legislator questioning the validity of one of his initiatives angrily declared, "In my part of the state we hung people for things like this." Bumphus respectfully replied, "Mr. Representative, they used to hang a lot of people, but not today." Talk about grace under pressure!

Bumphus' calming influence was evident during the aftermath of hurricanes Katrina and Rita as he worked with heads of the afflicted colleges. He led an arduous recovery effort that began with the development of a call center to re-establish critical internal and external communications and quickly organized temporary offices for the affected institutions. Working with his leadership team, Bumphus set up channels to ensure students and displaced employees received assistance after the storms.

**Difficult choices**

Coach Bob Huggins built the University of Cincinnati (UC) Bearcats into one of the more successful college basketball programs. He had a 399-127 record in 16 seasons and led the Bearcats to 14 straight NCAA tournaments. But Huggins' tenure was tarnished by his players' poor graduation rates and numerous off- court problems. Furthermore, National Collegiate Athletic Association (NCAA) probation and on-the-court demeanor, characterized by screaming at players and referees, did not help Huggins' cause. His behavior did not seem to bother alumni, students, fans, then-UC president Joseph Steiger, or even the athletic director who was Huggins' boss. They just cared that he won.

And then Huggins was arrested in June 2004 for a DUI. This infraction couldn't be overlooked by the new UC president, Nancy Zimpher, who vowed to act appropriately in raising the academic standards at the university. This included the basketball program as an aspect of her "UC 21 Plan."

A year later, Huggins was removed from his position amid outrage from his supporters—including some wealthy contributors who vowed to never give UC another dime if Huggins were not reinstated. Local newspapers, the *Cincinnati Enquirer* and the *Cincinnati Post*, carried praise for Mr. Huggins. Bars around campus sprouted signs that urged firing Zimpher.

She countered that she did not mind taking heat over Huggins. "My job is to articulate, as clearly as I possibly can, the future of this university and to get as many people moving together in that direction as possible," she said. "I am confident that an informed public knows exactly what I'm talking about."

In terminating Bob Huggins, Zimpher might have started the clock winding down on her own tenure at UC. Long after the incident, she was continually booed when attending university athletic events. In 2009, she was appointed Chancellor of the State University of New York, SUNY, by a board of trustees who applauded her handling of the Huggins' affair, and saw her restoring financial health at UC and raising its academic rank as evidence she would be a great fit for the new job.

### A real leader

Graham Jones, founder of Top Performance Consulting Limited, suggests that fortitude is perhaps what distinguishes real leaders from safe leaders. Safe leaders are so driven by their need for rewards, status, and power that there is little or no innovation or challenging of orthodoxy during their tenure. Their focus is almost exclusively on micro-managing the short term, often through exerting their status as the boss.

Real leaders are driven much more by the challenge and opportunity to make a difference. They are highly visible and make things happen. Their focus is much more on the future and the opportunities that lie ahead. Real leaders encourage innovation and risk-taking, as well as tackling hard issues as soon as they arise.

One real leader I had the privilege of knowing and serving a portion of my American Council of Education fellowship with was William Clyde Friday, a noted American educator who served for 30 years as the president of the multi-campus University of North Carolina.

Friday's biggest challenge during his tenure was addressing federal orders in 1970 to desegregate the system's 16 universities, five historically black and 11 predominantly white. The government proposed some aggressive and far-reaching measures, including the elimination of duplicate programs at traditionally white and black campuses to achieve racial balance. Representing a state that still held some segregationist leanings and housed conservative Republican U.S. Senator Jesse Helms, Friday advised moderation rather than the immediate introduction of the large changes demanded by Washington. The NAACP Legal Defense Fund called Friday's cautious response denial and defiance.

But Friday fought the government through the court system. The lawsuit was settled quietly with a consent decree that said, in effect, that between 1981 and 1986 UNC would be required to spend more money at historically black institutions. As the goal was educational equality for blacks, there were two areas to address. The first was integrating the traditionally white universities. The second was improving the quality of the traditionally black universities by increasing faculty with doctoral degrees and improving programs and facilities. To reach that settlement, Friday, a progressive and a liberal, had to work through challenging political environments at the state and national level. In 1986, the university system's board of governors voted voluntarily to continue compliance with decree commitments at all institutions, partly in honor of Friday, who retired in 1986.

Friday would come to be known for his skill as a behind-the-scenes mediator who worked to reconcile the priorities of the modern research university with the demands of a conservative and often intolerant state political establishment. The personal traits that would distinguish Friday's style of presidential leadership—integrity, indirect persuasion, a disarming sincerity, and a preference for consensus building through personal interaction in small groups—are ones that have stuck with me.

He molded the state's public colleges and universities into a single system, increased its student body more than eightfold, and was a force behind the creation of Research Triangle Park, a university-corporate collaboration that attracted high-tech industries to the Raleigh-Durham-Chapel Hill area.

These are just a few examples of great leaders in action who exemplify the tenets laid out in *Change the Lapel Pin*. As you undertake your journey, you will discover how to create your own leadership vision based on your ability to get along with individuals, interact with them, and, more importantly, understand their views. These examples are helpful as you encounter instances where your experience level may be insufficient. And I suspect there is no leader—whether existing or aspiring—who has not been influenced by something or someone.

Jacqueline Smith in "What Inspires the World's Top Leaders," summarized a poll completed by LinkedIn's Influencer Program, which asked selected leaders what inspired them. Some of the participants indicated that dedicated parents, in particular, and people like Walt Disney added joy and meaning to their personal and work lives. Among the respondents were Barack Obama, Arianna Huffington, and Sir Richard Branson. Branson said that his inspiration comes from game-changing people everywhere, who stop at nothing to make a positive difference in people's lives.

As you continually assess your individual encounters, it becomes apparent that inspiration can surface from almost anywhere. So never overlook an opportunity to enrich your leadership capacity and in so doing become the leader that people want to both emulate and follow.

# Acknowledging and Addressing Perils and Pitfalls

Even after you develop and refine your personalized approach, you can still expect challenges that must be prepared for, managed, and ameliorated. Earlier in the book, I referenced my awareness of several recent college presidencies which lasted only three to 18 months because of failures on the part of the individuals and organizations. Getting off to a good start is important and requires you to be stalwart in preparing for your leadership opportunity. The honeymoon period I described earlier is a chance to make a smooth transition to the organization and avoid the perils and pitfalls which can have a lasting effect on your progress. But even with a decent onboarding, it is probable that challenges may occur. And it is important to seek them out, acknowledge them, and resolve them directly. Let's consider some of the possibilities.

**Dubious vision and strategy**

As I have mentioned, developing your vision and strategies (one of your most important responsibilities) must be done with the involvement of key stakeholders. Without such collaboration, buy-in to actions you believe represent the best interests of the organization will not occur. Even when the vision and strategy are developed collaboratively, the actions or tactics to implement this duo still must be developed in partnership, since their achievement is dependent upon the work of individuals across the organization. Otherwise, you will not achieve the outcomes you anticipate.

Let's assume, though, you have done everything correctly.

You took the necessary steps to develop an outlook for the organization and worked collaboratively to develop the strategies and actions to reach this end. The work does not stop here. You must continue to repeatedly articulate their importance to ensure adherence. The results must be weighed to determine if they represent the outcomes you sought, can be sustained, or can serve as a foundation for future innovations. So, every aspect, from developing the vision to identifying the strategies and actions in response to it and measuring its success, requires widespread and continued involvement.

**Incomplete connections**

Achieving your vision and strategy is largely dependent upon ongoing communication and interaction with key stakeholders. As a college president who reports to a board of trustees, I made it a priority upon my arrival to determine their preferred method of communication. My first point of contact on any issue or concern is the chairman, who then makes the determination which of us should communicate with the other board members.

I also provide, without fail, weekly updates on college progress toward strategic priorities. Included in this report are press releases shared, first with the board so that they are not caught unaware when the stories are published.

Our regularly-scheduled, monthly meetings are preceded by a "targeted" discussion on policy and governance matters germane to the board, including student outcomes, financial and facility matters, and community outreach. Yearly retreats also consider these topics and permit the board to conduct and review its activities in concert with college operations.

As a new leader, if you report to a board of trustees or

equivalent oversight body, stay very close to your board chair to ensure your early actions are consistent and appropriate with her and the full board's expectations.

Refrain from discussing board issues with your employees. It is inappropriate to engage in and welcome such conversations. And you may not be aware upon your arrival of the connections between your employees and board members.

Another area where ongoing communication is imperative is with key leaders of constituent groups. They can help you expand the lines of communication, provide advice and leadership on strategic priorities, and help to both identify and resolve issues. Having these relationships throughout my various presidencies has been educational and rewarding.

At two of the three institutions where I served, the faculty were unionized and had attendant bodies called faculty senates that dealt with instructional quality and integrity. The third college had a group called the "Federation," which essentially acted as a quasi-bargaining group. I met regularly with leaders to obtain information on the mood of their colleagues, foster our vision for student excellence, and seek their input and leadership on the various strategies needed to accomplish the vision. I conveyed publicly my deep respect and admiration for their staunch advocacy and determined commitment to their constituents.

In all instances, the leaders were principled professionals who were not only interested in securing benefits for their colleagues, but, like me, were committed to heightening the faculty role in increasing educational attainment of students inside the classroom and beyond. This is where we reached an accord that fostered meaningful collaboration among all groups at the college.

**Lack of transparency**

You must be willing and able to regularly convey the status of the organization, its successes and its challenges. The exception, of course, concerns a legal or policy matter—such as those affecting property and personnel—which require discretion and confidentiality. But when routine operations are unclear or shrouded in secrecy, concerns about transparency and consistency rise and morale plummets.

It is important, then, that you be cognizant of the necessity to be open when practicable and always honest. Integrity is an important and expected attribute in a leader that can be strengthened through clear, consistent, and regular communications on the purpose and direction of the organization. A rationale for important decisions is an important element to increase accountability. It also helps when roles and responsibilities are clearly defined.

**Concern for individual convenience over organizational advancement**

An area where leaders may falter is when they focus on the comfort of an individual, or themselves, over the interests of the organization. In this regard, personnel decisions generally can be among the most impactful actions that a leader can take for advancing the aims of the organization, especially when new employees are properly oriented and understand their roles. The hiring process should not be shrouded in secrecy to the extent it leads to concerns about transparency. The process should be a joint effort; open, honest, and explainable, especially when an individual is selected without a formal search.

When a formal search is conducted, however, the responsibility of a screening committee is to recommend candidates based on the job description. Diverse viewpoints and backgrounds can be taken into consideration, along with demonstrated competencies and fit. The fact that an individual comes through as likeable, while important, should not constitute the primary reason for a hiring recommendation.

The evaluation of employees is an important tool for guiding the performance and development of people. As baby boomers retire and the workforce is comprised of subsequent generations, organizations will need to shift the focus of the workplace and evaluations, in part, from individuals to teams and projects where leadership is both identified and nurtured essentially at the ground level.

The time comes for every leader when they must make difficult choices that affect people they have come to know professionally and personally. These individuals may not be performing maximally in an important role but they are pleasant to work with. Being pleasant is fine, but it does not trump productivity. Make no mistake, your employees watch these situations to determine how you will address them.

Once you have determined your course of action, act swiftly. You can separate people immediately, place someone on a 30 to 90-day day performance improvement plan, or place them in another position in the organization where their talents and skills might be a better match.

Be careful, however, if you exercise the latter two options. If performance continues to be unacceptable, you have no choice but to curtail employment. Not doing so would imply that you are shifting dead weight or could be viewed as you being incapable of making a difficult choice. Neither situation is one you want to find yourself in—your ability to lead will be compromised.

Then there is the situation where you have a productive employee who disagrees with their supervisor whom you know has been an issue for a while. The disgruntled employee is seeking a transfer to another area of the organization where they can report to someone else. This presents a difficult choice for any leader. The supervisor should have been dealt with earlier. But addressing the situation after-the-fact is not plausible either, since any action against the supervisor would appear to be caused by the employee's complaints.

I have previously encountered this situation. My decision was to not move the employee to another area, and this response led to her resignation. I hated to lose such a valuable colleague, but it allowed me to finally address the supervisor's incompetence.

He was separated from the college, which was not taken kindly by some of his colleagues, as he was a long-time employee and well-liked. In his place, I secured a more accomplished and personable individual, and the area in question became among the most productive at the college I was leading at the time.

## Lack of experience

On occasion, there are situations that materialize where experience is necessary. Experience counts. But inexperienced leaders have options they can apply in these instances when they lack experience in the cycles and/or the art of leadership or when their intuition is immature.

**Incomplete cycle of leadership.** A good friend and supervisor, Dr. Callie Coaxum, once told me that knowing the cycles of leadership can be an important tool in dealing with a current issue—even if it only approximates what you have experienced.

But what happens when your leadership experience has not come full circle? What happens when you encounter an unusual event?

First, do not overreact. Take your time when confronting something you are not familiar with. This can become an important ally that allows you to deliberate, using your education and experience to identify the most appropriate solutions. Call upon a trusted advisor to determine if your response is plausible.

Another option is to seek out the views of leaders within the organization, although they may not report to you or carry a formal title. The use of this method assumes you have developed a relationship built on mutual trust and loyalty with the individual you seek out.

One caution, remember you assume full responsibility for the outcomes, regardless of who you consulted.

**Underplaying the art of leadership.** Bill Friday, the beloved president of the University of North Carolina, was perhaps the poster child for the art of leadership. He once told me that the "best way to maintain and build power, is never to use it."

So, what does this mean? It means your work is accomplished best without reliance on positional or titular power—that which is associated with your leadership role. As you might recall from Friday's portrait of leadership, in 1971 Friday had to lead the desegregation of the University of North Carolina system amid immense federal government pressure in a state noted, even today, for its discriminatory leanings. While Friday wielded positional power, it did not compare with a state political system hell-bent on maintaining the status quo.

So, Friday relied on what I refer to as relational power. He applied personal attributes—integrity, indirect persuasion, a disarming sincerity, and a preference for consensus building through personal interaction in small groups—to develop a solution that was acceptable to federal and state politicians.

Relational power is, perhaps, the most difficult for a new leader to establish. Novice leaders often depend first on positional power to address challenges, mostly in isolation and without the benefit of consultation.

More often, however, mature leaders depend first on personal attributes, coalitions, humility, and consensus-building. Then they apply the solution.

My advice is that new leaders combine the benefits of positional and relational power in decision-making.

**Immature wisdom.** Alongside knowledge is wisdom. Though less applied and more tacit in nature, wisdom is an important tool; sensing what is going on through subtleties that signal a much more deeply-rooted concern, most dealing with four distinct areas: insufficient connections, absence of transparency, lack of respect and appreciation, and poor communications. Some veteran leaders recognize early the impact of even the smallest concern in any one of these areas and move quickly to resolve it through mechanisms already in place.

New leaders are usually focused on transitioning to the new role and all it entails. And therefore, their wisdom may be less advanced at a critical time. Despite your obligations, it is important to become attuned to the intricacies of the organization.

Earlier in the book, I talked about being observant, noticing details and recognizing patterns can help you be proactive earlier in addressing challenges and responding to trends. This greater awareness takes time to develop. But when established, you will be equipped to more readily identify the salient-yet-critical issues that must be addressed before they become hazardous to you and your organization.

*Relational power is, perhaps, the most difficult for a new leader to establish.*

## Callie Coaxum, wise and principled leader

An individual who ably dealt with a difficult environment in a wise and principled fashion was the aforementioned Callie Coaxum. Coaxum, considered an outsider, was elevated on an interim basis to the second-highest executive-level position at Winston-Salem State University (WSSU) over longer serving administrators who initially rebuffed nearly every decision she made.

She could not relieve all these individuals from their positions at once. She received no help from her supervisor—who soon left for another presidency. So, she decided to involve her critics in responding to a source of embarrassment for the university, which was the poor performance of first-year students. Coaxum's effort resulted in some important programs and outcomes, including higher grade point averages for students and their increased retention through the second year.

Despite these achievements, Coaxum was not considered for the permanent position by WSSU's new leader. Her replacement was roundly criticized by her former detractors for his ineffectiveness and was replaced after just two years. By this time, however, Coaxum had departed to a great position at Fayetteville State University. I was eventually chosen for the vacant position at WSSU, in which I served for six years before moving on to Cuyahoga Community College for the first time in 1993.

Coaxum was my supervisor during my first administrative post at WSSU, from 1983 to 1985. I could not have been paired with a better role model for professional decorum. She was a wise and ethical person who would not compromise her character for anyone.

As leaders, we are often compelled to work around the margins of our integrity. The solutions in these instances seldom have lasting value. They erode trust that ultimately cannot be regained. And worse, they can compromise the organization.

Coaxum taught me that being principled starts with assessing your own value system to ensure your fortitude is sufficient to uphold your integrity and that of the organization. This notion begins with open and honest dialogue.

So, when difficulty appears—and it will—it will not result in surprise and panic, which can weaken your connection with individuals. In the process, you become experienced and gain wisdom that can be applied in all types of situations.

I have faced adversity numerous times as a president. But even during the moments I was almost completely surprised by a situation—and yes, this will happen to you—because I practiced what Coaxum represented, the organization was able to deal with it and recover. It is infinitely better as in the case of a budget reduction or layoff, that individuals be consulted and updated on the solutions.

Here's just one example: The Community College of Allegheny County, where I served as president from 2008 to 2013, was financially strapped because of diminished funding from the Commonwealth of Pennsylvania and the county. We could not increase tuition, which already represented nearly 50 percent of the annual revenue (in contrast, at Cuyahoga the percentage is 24).

Among the options for responding to this financial shortfall was to outsource costly book store operations to a vendor.

We created a team of stakeholders—including several leaders of the union representing the employees affected by the action.

The team developed a list of requirements for a vendor. These included continued employment of qualified staff, updated and modernized bookstores, and a scholarship fund.

The terms were acceptable to one company, but when placed before the union—as required by the state—it was not approved. A second vote, however, approved the agreement when all staff were promised continued membership in the union.

There is probably no way to escape perils and pitfalls. They are everywhere. To mitigate them, however, it is important to ensure that the areas of possible conflict discussed earlier are addressed and specific principles are in place.

Lynn Offermann offers some additional advice in her article, "When Followers Become Toxic":

- **Keep vision and values front and center.** It is much easier to get sidetracked when you are unclear about what the main track is.
- **Make sure people continue to disagree and debate.** Remember that most of us form opinions too quickly and give them up too slowly.
- **Cultivate truth tellers.** Make sure there are people in

your world you can trust to tell you what you need to hear—no matter how unpopular or unpalatable the truth is.

- **Do as you would have done to you.** Followers look to what you do rather than what you say. Set a good ethical climate for your team to be sure your followers have clear boundaries for their actions.
- **Honor your intuition.** If you think you have a challenge, you are probably right.
- **Delegate, do not desert.** It is important to share control and empower your staff, but remember who's ultimately responsible for the outcome.

# Diversity as a Condition for Success Global Economy

In this section I expand upon my stated belief that individuals from varied backgrounds should get a chance to attain the American Dream of prosperity and enlightened citizenship. My desire here also is to help leaders understand their role in making this happen in a world increasingly dependent upon a skilled and diverse workforce.

Diversity has advanced beyond its historic position as a focus and outcome of America's civil rights movement. It is *still* an important tool for achieving equality and mitigating the vestiges of discrimination. And, it has become also a powerful reminder that acknowledging and celebrating differences among people is healthy and rewarding for promoting both social equality and business through workplace diversity, which refers to the variety of differences between people in an organization.

So, it has to do with more than race or ethnicity. Gender, sexual orientation, cognitive style, tenure, organizational function, education, background and more are included in the definition. And, it is the strengths and talents of this combination who will, as Harvard University professors David Thomas and Robin Ely suggests, assist in developing an outlook on diversity that contributes to the organization by rethinking primary tasks and redefining markets, products, strategies, missions, business practices, and even cultures.

This observation offered by Thomas and Ely is important to organizational development as the presence of diverse workers continues to climb. In America today, more than 36 percent of the labor force is comprised of workers from different ethnic and racial backgrounds. This percentage is projected to grow so that by 2050 there will be no racial or ethnic majority in the workplace. These statistics are being fueled, in part, by an increasing multi-cultural population and globalization, which require creativity and openness to change in a worldwide economy that is replacing an insular marketplace.

Another trend fueling a diverse workforce is the advancements in technology as an indispensable business and personal necessity, requiring organizations to look for workers beyond America, where the gap between available jobs and skilled workers is immense. This shortage is apparent within the technical, professional, and supervisory ranks and the gap is widening as businesses themselves, and colleges like Cuyahoga, implement training programs for prospective and incumbent workers to overcome the shortfall.

### Advantages and challenges of a diverse workplace

An organization's success and competitiveness in the future depend upon its willingness to embrace diversity and its benefits, which happens when organizations actively assess their desire to establish a varied workplace and develop and implement plans and strategies for achieving it. These advantages include the availability of a more talented workforce, the presence of different viewpoints, and the existence of a more affirming culture for customers.

*Diversity has advanced beyond its historic position as a focus and outcome of America's civil rights movement.*

On a personal level, learning about different lifestyles and cultures can be an important outcome.

This perspective contributes to an inclusive environment that understands the needs of their employees, makes them feel valued and respected, and contributes to retention. Perhaps most importantly, companies that openly articulate values of inclusion tend to appeal to a wider customer and supplier base. In short, both diversity and inclusion are good for the worker and the business.

But developing a workplace that actively seeks out and applies the viewpoints of diverse individuals and groups is challenging. While strides were made during the last half-century to rid the country of a long history of discrimination, eliminating the remnants of this period exemplified by the expanding economic and social gulf has been more difficult. And in fact, some Americans report race relations in the U.S. have deteriorated, based a poll conducted in 2015 by PBS News Hour and Marist College's Institute for Public Opinion.

The 2016 presidential campaign did little to lessen this climate, as both sides engaged in rhetoric that may have contributed to the slippage. Josh Greenberg, in "Diversity in the Workplace: Benefits, Challenges and Solutions," believes that Hillary Clinton's description of Donald Trump supporters as a "basket of deplorables," may have sparked increased prejudice and paranoia already evident in a fraction of his base and created a bigger platform for their views and voices. Trump's generalized depiction of illegal residents from Mexico fed his base, but also enraged zealous Clinton supporters. I could go on describing other very public incidents that have fueled intolerance, but I have made my point that the extent diversity is embraced (or rejected) is often dependent upon the beliefs of the leader, whether of a country or an organization.

In addition to a polarized nation, also possibly effecting the extent that you can assemble a diverse workforce are factors within organizations. Greenberg provided the following examples:

- **Communication.** Perceptual, cultural, and language barriers need to be overcome for diversity programs to succeed. Ineffective communication of key objectives results in confusion, lack of teamwork, and low morale.
- **Resistance to change.** There are always employees who will refuse to accept the fact that the social and cultural makeup of their workplace is changing. The "we've always done it this way" mentality silences new ideas and inhibits progress.
- **Implementation of diversity in the workplace policies**. This can be the overriding challenge to all diversity advocates. Armed with the results of employee assessments and research data, they must build and implement a customized strategy to maximize the effects of diversity in the workplace for their organization.
- **Management of diversity in the workplace.** Diversity training alone is not sufficient for your organization's diversity management plan. A strategy must be created and implemented to create a culture of diversity that permeates every department and function of the organization.

When you add these challenges, along with the climate in the country, it makes the job of creating a more diverse-conscious workplace difficult. But there is no countering the future trend that will lead to a more multicultural society and workforce. Either we embrace and benefit from this reality or ignore it to the detriment of the country.

On the job, attempts to increase diversity through only a focus on compliance with government rules and regulations have backfired, sometimes even heightening tensions among employees and hindering a company's performance. Rather than concentrating solely on recruitment and retention goals, Thomas and Ely conclude that organizations should incorporate cultural and personal perspectives of employees into the main work of the organization. This inclusionary "learning-and-effectiveness paradigm," according to the researchers, taps into diversity's true benefits.

But there are certain preconditions that help to position organizations to apply this approach successfully. These include:

- Understanding a diverse workforce embodies different perspectives and approaches to work and truly values the variety of opinions and insights people with different cultural backgrounds bring to the organization.
- Recognizing the opportunities and challenges diversity presents to the organization, embracing them, and committing to finding healthy ways they contribute to organizational learning, growth, and renewal.
- In the organizational culture, creating expectations of high standards of performance from everyone, regardless of their racial or ethnic background. These are reinforced through training and education programs that nurture personal development and through carefully designed jobs that maximize the potential of people without relegating them to isolated niche areas within the organization.

- Making individuals feel valued and encouraged to apply their background and skills in creative ways to improve the work of the organization unencumbered by unnecessary bureaucratic systems that limit diversity and inclusion.

### Exemplary diversity programs

Do companies readily embrace diversity, even when they claim to make it a part of company culture and business operations? According to DiversityInc, one way to judge this is through external measures. Each year since 2001, the company has published a list of the top corporations noted to understand and promulgate the business value of diversity management through best practices that other companies adapt to improve their efforts. Across top companies identified by DiversityInc, some common themes emerged.

**CEOs directly involved.** While many companies have chief diversity officers, or a head of human resources, who oversees diversity efforts, those that stand out are the ones where the CEO is actively engaged. AT&T Chairman and CEO Randall Stephenson heads the company's executive diversity council and founded it in 2008.

**Technology as a diversity tool.** Companies are using technology platforms to facilitate diversity and mentoring programs. Johnson & Johnson, for example, has a custom web-enabled service called Mentoring Works!, along with the Johnson & Johnson Diversity University, an online resource to help employees build diversity into collaborative efforts.

**Affinity groups.** Companies create affinity or business resource groups for workers that fit into a variety of categories. Prudential has seven business resource groups,

including Abled and Disabled Associates Partnering
Together (ADAPT), Prudential Military Veterans Network
(VETNET), Employee Association of Gay Men, Lesbians,
Bisexual, Transgender and Allies (EAGLES), and the newest,
Generations, which focuses on generational diversity.

**Flexible working environment.** While there has been a
recent trend away from telecommuting as part of corporate
culture—made most notable by former Yahoo CEO Marissa
Mayer's decision to not allow Yahoo employees to work from
home—most of the companies on the DiversityInc list have
flexible work policies as part of diversity efforts.

**Supplier diversity.** Companies require suppliers to
incorporate their own diversity values and even compensate
supply-chain executives based on diversity goals. Procter
& Gamble has an executive compensation plan tied to
successful completion of staff and supplier diversity
initiatives.

Despite these notable examples, companies themselves
realize there is work to be done to achieve true workplace
diversity. This means that the leader can no longer model
and assume behavior, it must be institutionalized. Even
in the DiversityInc top 50 are corporation involved in
lawsuits: Novartis for gender discrimination; AT&T for
racial discrimination; and Apple on multiple discrimination
charges.

Allegations of venture capitalists sexually harassing
women tech entrepreneurs is among the latest revelations
to possibly impede achievement of diversity at the heights
of corporate America. During this controversy, reported
by *CNN Tech*, two powerful Silicon Valley investors, Dave
McClure of 500 Startups and Justin Caldbeck of Binary

Capital, resigned and issued broad apologies for their sexual misconduct against females seeking work or venture capital. Most firms making investment decision are headed by men, and in 2016 these companies contributed $64.9 billion into male-founded startups, compared to $1.5 billion into female-headed ventures.

This incident was followed by fallout at Google (supposedly one of the most diversity conscious companies among the tech giants) when one of its engineers published "Google's Ideological Echo Chamber," which promoted "ideological" rather than gender diversity and contended women do not make up 50 percent of the company's tech and leadership positions because of differences in their preferences and abilities, not sexism. According to Elizabeth Weise and John Swartz of *USA Today*, this sentiment underscores the views of many at tech companies who do not agree with the diversity mandate of employers like Google. They counter that Silicon Valley is a meritocracy, where brilliance and talent are consistently rewarded above all else, sometimes without recognizing that the same attributes exist among older adults, women, and minorities.

Board of Director diversity is another area of concern. According to DiversityInc, even the most progressive companies struggle with Board makeup even though it recently reached an all-time high for Fortune 500 companies according to a report issued by Deloitte and the Alliance for Board Diversity. In 2016, women and minorities occupied about 31 percent of the board seats of Fortune 500 companies—an increase from 25.5 percent in 2010 and 26.7 percent in 2012. Despite an increase in diversity, boards are still 79.8 percent male.

Politics have also crept into the conversation.

Organizations need to be careful of who and what they back. More corporate leaders are weighing in on issues typically heralded by politicians and advocacy groups. High profile CEOs who think strategically can persuade others through direct discussion, networking, and influence. However, these acts have potential consequences that did not exist years ago because we are a more inter-connected world.

Organizations, specifically their leaders, must better understand the attitudes of internal and external stakeholders when it comes to controversial issues. An online survey conducted by Weber Shandwick and KRC Research found activism not directly linked to the organization's fundamental business is not a good idea. Respondents said they are less likely to buy from a company whose stance on an issue they disagree with. However, one of the most interesting findings was that in some cases, activism works when it is designed around attracting media attention, to build a CEO's reputation, or to sell more products or services to a specific group.

Another challenge, described by Allison Gordon, is "cross-generational transfer of knowledge and culture." As baby boomers remain in the workforce longer, the difference between this generation and the next becomes blatantly apparent. I will discuss this phenomenon in the section entitled "The Future of Leadership." But briefly, cultural difference can be a challenge as younger workers approach work differently, use technology more readily, and may not be as committed to the culture and history of a company. These aspects should be transmitted by older workers so that younger employees do not miss out on understanding important structural aspects and values, concluded Julie Goodridge, CEO of NorthStar Asset Management.

**Higher education as a source for a diverse workforce**
The preparation of a diverse workforce is a high priority. Although some companies have established their own training programs, they do not often award credentials that are transferable to a different occupation or job. For this reason, and to draw upon the efficiency and expertise available at colleges and universities, employers should continue to rely upon the nation's postsecondary institutions for preparing workers.

Historically, higher education has been the laboratory for social equality. As such, it serves as an example for corporations that are more recent proponents of diversity and inclusion. For instance, before colleges exclusively for African Americans, like Fisk University and Howard University, were opened following the Civil War, black students enrolled at institutions including Oberlin College and Conservatory as early as 1833.

Today, the practice of diversity in higher education is no longer just a commitment to social consciousness, but has become an obligation to develop individuals, regardless of background, who contribute as citizens and leaders to the economy of the country and its democratic ideals. This notion is echoed in a report from the American Council on Education, *A Matter of Excellence: A Guide to Strategic Diversity Leadership and Accountability in Higher Education,* which concludes that diversity on college campuses is no longer just a question of moral and social responsibility.

It is critical to enabling students to achieve excellence and gain competitive advantages in the 21st century knowledge economy, as demonstrated in the following chart on the following page.

## Higher Education Role in Creating a Diverse Workforce

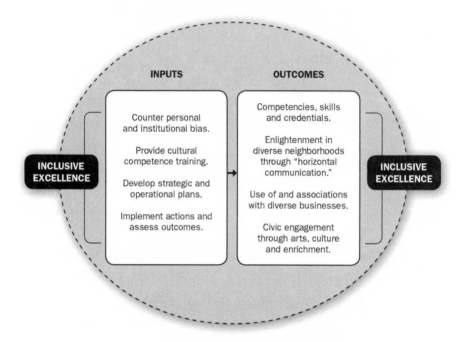

In higher education, the concept of Inclusive Excellence, introduced by the Association of American Colleges and Universities (AAC&U) expands upon the principles proposed in *Matter of Excellence* that foster diversity in the college, workplace, and community. By integrating Inclusive Excellence into their operations, equity and educational quality becomes an active process by which colleges and universities achieve distinction in everything they do. This result requires them to uncover gaps in educational attainment throughout student groups, identify effective educational practices to eliminate them, and build practices organically for sustained institutional change that spills over into the community. According to *Matter of Excellence*, the framework for this effort is strategic diversity leadership and systems of accountability and performance management that position the diversity and inclusion program at the highest level of the organization.

No sector of higher education is better equipped to assume the responsibility of preparing a diverse, technically trained workforce than community colleges. Their student populations are extremely varied. According to the American Association of Community Colleges (AACC), 45 percent of undergraduates in higher education attend community colleges, including 62 percent of Native Americans, 57 percent of Hispanics, and 52 percent of Blacks. By gender, community college enrollment is 57 percent women, 36 percent for first generation students.

With this varied student population, combined with a diverse employee base—even at the upper echelons of the organizations as presidents and vice presidents—and inclusive environments, two-year institutions are infinitely prepared for the tailored, intentional, and (in some instances) mandatory educational experiences that increase success and expedite graduation for all students.

Many community college leaders have aggressively sought to ensure that diverse student populations reap the benefits of attending their institutions. In concert with Inclusive Excellence, the approach at Cuyahoga emphasizes purposeful development and utilization of resources to enhance learning, emphasizing a welcoming community where achieving equity is everyone's responsibility.

Professional development focused on understanding the needs of students from different cultural backgrounds is key. This takes place in many forms, including college-wide gatherings, like an Equity Summit that mirrored the "big idea" concept perfected by Valencia College president Sandy Shugart. As I explained in the section of this book called "Words Matter," Shugart is a proponent of convening upwards of 200 people in a room to analyze a specific topic. After a set time, they reconvene, review their responses and repeat the small-group sessions to reach accord. It's a technique designed to immediately reach a strong set of ideas that are actionable.

The Equity Summit at Cuyahoga helped the existing Equity Task Force (comprised of a cross-section of the college community) propose college-wide actions to be implemented on each of the four campuses by their Success Teams. These actions include, in part, purposeful and inescapable programs and other specialized services, such as mentoring from the Hispanic Council, the Black American Council, and other organizations. Thus, enabling students to graduate timelier and in increasing numbers using an individualized case management approach. This is one of the major strategic initiatives of Cuyahoga's Access, Learning, and Success division, which is responsible directly for student learning and development.

These programs of value allow students to transfer seamlessly to four-year institutions to complete bachelor's degrees or to satisfy the requirements for a credential permitting them to compete for the growing number of jobs that require high tech skills and provide a family-sustaining wage. But for those prospects to be available to higher numbers of individuals from poor and minority communities, the two-year sector must expand its access portal.

At Cuyahoga, some of this responsibility falls on the shoulders of my colleagues in Cuyahoga's Workforce Community and Economic Development division. This division has associations and partnerships with more than 300 community groups and organizations whose purpose is to provide unfettered access to the colleges for underserved groups and neighborhoods.

In each of the six Centers of Excellence named below, there are programs that support this aim by helping individuals develop competencies and earn certificates or degrees. The centers are registering some impressive outcomes, including improved scores on licensure examinations, apprenticeships and other pre-job experiences, employment, and increased visibility. The six centers and initiatives for diverse student populations are described on the following pages.

**Creative Arts.** Academies provided in conjunction with the Boys and Girls Club and the Cleveland Metropolitan School District, and funded by the Cleveland Foundation, offer classical and jazz music and dance classes for youth as early as the third grade.

**Hospitality Management.** Many opportunities, such as the Hospitality Boot Camp, get individuals started on their education and, simultaneously, prepared for a job in Cleveland's expansive hotel and restaurant sector.

**Manufacturing Technology.** The "Right Skills Now" program with Swagelok, Incorporated is an eight to 10-week program in "clean" manufacturing that provides great wages and benefits with an expanding company. The Construction Diversity Initiative (CDI) prepares individuals for membership in the construction trades or employment at a key Cleveland employer, including the Cleveland Clinic, University Hospitals, the Sewer District, and construction firms, like Turner.

**Nursing.** The TEAMSS (Targeting Educational Assistance for Minority Student Success) program, funded by a federal grant from the Health Resources Services Administration (HRSA), provides stipends, educational support, and other resources that help minority students overcome barriers to their education.

**Public Safety.** An endowment from KeyBank provides scholarship for youth from the city's diverse neighborhoods and summer programs to be exposed to prospective careers such as police officers, emergency responders/technicians, and firefighters.

**Information Technology.** Boot camps like Cleveland Codes are an affordable way for individuals to develop skills for entry level positions and a chance to continue their education funded by the employer.

Despite these attainments, Cuyahoga and other community colleges must improve the production of more technically skilled graduates from diverse backgrounds. At Cuyahoga, this is an institution-wide responsibility coinciding with the tenets of Inclusive Excellence. The classroom provides perspectives on life in a multicultural society, which benefits students and where they live directly, especially when they share knowledge and understanding with their neighbors, friends, and co-workers about the true value of diversity. This "horizontal communication" on the part of students emerges when interactions in the college allow them to gain perspectives of the world they can share in their networks and neighborhoods. They also develop a more complete view of the workplace and their place in a global society, according to Jeremy Hyman and Lynn Jacobs in "Why Does Diversity Matter at College Anyway?"

Inclusive Excellence also expands the benefit of diversity and inclusion to the community. Often these efforts involve collaborations with community groups and organizations for cultural arts offerings, enrichment programs for school-age children, and activities for retirees. For example, Encore is an affordable program for retirees that allows them to experience a wide range of specially designed seminars and recreational activities. I have already mentioned Cuyahoga coordinated in 2017 "Stokes: Honoring the Past, Inspiring the Future," which was a year-long commemoration of the 50th Anniversary of the election of Carl Stokes as the first African American mayor of a major U.S. city, Cleveland, and the contributions of his brother, Congressman Louis Stokes. This is another way that the benefits of Inclusive Excellence are serving the greater good.

And, like the corporations recognized by DiversityInc, supplier diversity has become important in higher education, especially for public institutions that receive government funding. There is an expectation these colleges and universities attempt to conduct business with diverse enterprises to bring higher ROI to a broader cross-section of the community. In support of this aim, Cuyahoga adopted a five-year plan, 2017-2022, designed to expand supplier, professional services, and construction diversity with specific goals and benchmarks whose attainment is dependent upon outreach to ensure that company's know how to do business with the college.

Based on what has been covered in this section, how do you as a leader, regardless of the organization, make the benefits of diversity evident?

You must first confront your own biases and those of your colleagues. Provide training on cultural sensitivity for them and you. These first steps make it possible to recognize and change institutional practices that present barriers and to implement an approach where diversity is threaded throughout the organization. With this foundation, it is easier to lead the development of an organization-wide effort with the following requirements.

Next, ensure that the organizational framework is solid strategically and operationally and that diversity is an integral component of every unit. A firmly structured organization with diversity as a core value encourages employees to contribute to organizational goals, promote diversity as a business necessity, and embrace social responsibility and community engagement. These demonstrated benefits allow you to more readily address underrepresentation and bring into the organization other talented individuals, perhaps with different ideas and perspectives. These individuals form resource groups that, for example, hold regular events and advocate for diversity awareness. Publicizing your commitment may expand your customer base in the communities you serve and help

uncover suppliers that are also committed to diversity.
During this effort, you develop a reputation as an employer
of choice.

From a purely social perspective, the level of acceptance
for individuals from diverse backgrounds is imperative as
our nation continues to become more color neutral. Taken
to a larger context, including the economic advantage,
experiencing diversity is essential as our workforce rapidly
continues to represent more minority groups. According
to the Center for American Progress, half of our nation's
workforce will soon be comprised of minorities. And with
the economic future of our country resting squarely in the
hands of this rapidly growing population, it is essential
that today's college students develop as productive and
knowledgeable citizens living in a multicultural world.

## Howard Schultz, model of leadership, committed to diversity and inclusion

A leader who overwhelmingly understands the benefits of
a multicultural workforce and society is Howard Schultz,
former CEO, and now Chairman, of Starbucks and one of
the most visible chief executives in the country. He believes
there is no difference between work and education and the
combination is a powerful inducement for helping poor and
minority individuals achieve the American Dream.

Schultz has made Starbucks a vocal part of the national
conversation on issues like gun violence, gay rights, race
relations, veterans rights, and student debt. Besides building
a diverse workforce and providing them with a full-range of
benefits, including health care and funds for college, whether
you are a full or part time employee, Schultz believes the
power of corporations like his should be to "inspire and
nurture the human spirit" across America. Nothing is more

emblematic of this sentiment than a letter to his colleagues dated January 29, 2017, wherein he promised to support the participants in DACA, the Deferred Action of Childhood Arrivals program, announced an initiative to hire 10,000 refugees, and vowed to protect the Starbucks customers and workers in Mexico through an initiative entitled "Building Bridges, Not Walls, with Mexico."

Schultz's most controversial attempt to promote dialog amid simmering racial tensions in America was "Race Together," essentially a statement designed to ignite conversation written on customer's cups by baristas. The campaign's opponents charged that such a sensitive cultural topic was too complex to be introduced in coffee shop lines by individuals with no expertise in the area. To illustrate their objection, they referred to photos that only featured white baristas holding cups bearing the hand-written "Race Together" message. "Race Together" was halted. But according to Andrew Sorkin of the *New York Times,* the ever-relentless Schultz contended upon its withdrawal that the intent was to maintain Starbucks' moral courage, elevate the national conversation, and challenge the status quo about the role of a public company.

Schultz's evolution is not unlike many of the *Change the Lapel Pin* leaders profiled in this book. Leaders whose experiences, education, and exposures have served as the platform for their success. Schultz grew up in public housing located in the blue-collar Canarsie section of Brooklyn. When he was 7 years old, his father broke a foot on the job but had no health insurance or worker's compensation. According to Shana Lenowitz of *Business Insider,* in a way Schultz believed his tremendous professional success is a tribute to his father who "never attained fulfillment and dignity from work he found meaningful." Schultz realized his future needed to be different than his parents. So, after graduating from Northern Michigan University and holding several jobs, Schultz encountered Starbucks when he was working for a manufacturer of drip coffee makers. He eventually met Starbuck owners Gerald Baldwin and Gordon Bowker and was so taken with their passion and courage that he went to work for them and eventually purchased the company in 1987 for $3.8 million. Today, Starbucks is valued at an estimated $84.6 billion, and Schultz's net worth is at least $3 billion.

# The Future of Leadership

It was my objective in writing *Change the Lapel Pin: Personalizing Leadership to Transform Organizations and Communities* to equip you with the knowledge on how to succeed in a leadership position. I hoped, too, that you would learn how to develop a personalized approach that you create and nourish well into the future based on the Three Essentials—education, experience, and exposure. This hope persists even though it is difficult to know exactly what leadership might look like in the near future. George Vielmeete and Yvonne Sele share this viewpoint as well, based on an exhaustive study detailed in their book *Leadership 2030*. The authors do agree, however, that certain trends in business will be dramatically different in the future and, as a result, may impact the way people and organizations are led. Following are some examples of their findings:

- Despite attempts in the United States to contain businesses, a new economic world order is emerging. Power is shifting to fast-developing markets in Asia (China, in particular) and away from "old" global markets.
- People will come to expect their individual needs to be catered to. This will create niche opportunities for customized offerings, diversify the demands of employees, and require far greater sensitivity and agility from organizations.
- Living and working with digital technology is becoming the norm. Digital platforms are shifting to employees and breaking down old divisions between

personal and professional life. The wave of technology innovation will create new product markets and require businesses to stay ahead of the curve through research and development programs.

- A burgeoning and rapidly aging world population will transform markets. This will result in a shrinking global workforce, sparking a war for talent among organizations on an unprecedented scale. Leaders will need to cope with the demands of an increasingly intergenerational workforce, in which each age group has vastly diverse attitudes and requirements.

And I am sure that there will be other occurrences that impact how organizations conduct business, some political in nature. For example, an event worth mentioning is the 2016 election of Donald John Trump as President of the United States. Some of his campaign promises, such as repealing the Affordable Care Act, limiting immigration, and renegotiating the North America Free Trade Agreement (NAFTA) are laboring due to extraneous matters—especially an investigation into whether Russia interfered with the 2016 presidential election—and may have an impact that is yet-to-be-determined.

**The future of work and leadership**
In view of these trends, the need for agility to create a competitive advantage is requiring organizations and people to change. In this environment, according to Peter Cappelli and Anna Travis in "The Performance Management Revolution," teamwork is preferred where customer service demands that frontline and back-office employees, for example, work together. Making it more effective when the team is allowed to solve problems to improve performance and develop skills for the future. As projects—rather than

chores—are implemented, employees become accustomed to working in teams on shorter-duration jobs.

It will be important to focus on people development because the talent market has tightened, making competition for skilled workers stiff. It will become much more critical to create and nurture a work environment where individuals understand how professional development can be gratifying to themselves and the organization and realize their contributions can lead to advancement on jobs either inside or outside the organization.

Some of the most talented of the next generation will seek to work in settings that accommodate their preference for social media and the Internet. They may aspire to have jobs that focus on projects as opposed to those that are routine and repetitive, seek a work/life balance where each element is viewed equally, and choose to use their private time to personally support worthy causes. As a result, there is greater pressure on organizations to build a compelling employer brand that reflects these values at every level of the organization so they are perceived as consistent, pervasive, and genuine. By embracing these talented generations, organizations will improve their teams and add new vitality to their cultures.

Leaders will emerge from this workforce who transfer the characteristics of the group to their new capacities. According to Jacob Morgan of the Future of Work Community, these leaders will present new attitudes, expectations, and ways of thinking that will transform the workplace. Harnessing and developing the talent of subsequent generations will be critical as they ascend to leadership positions while baby boomers retire in higher percentages during the years to come. This generation of future leaders will tend to be an enormously collaborative group that finds strength and purpose in working together towards common goals. Their inclusionary nature means they are less inclined to blindly follow orders and more comfortable understanding the big picture and their part in it, according to J. Walker Smith and Ann Cluma.

Prospective leaders will be a cohort of digital natives—they have essentially used technology and the many forms of communication it affords since birth. This group is used to having instant access to information and continually processes it using YouTube and other video platforms. Just as with their Generation X and baby boomer predecessors, Millennials are keenly aware of what they don't know and are desperate to find a trusted veteran to offer guidance.

The following chart depicts some key characteristics of Millennials, based on a list developed by Digitalist, "The Rise of Millennials in Leadership Roles."

| Attribute | Millennials |
|---|---|
| Leadership | 40 percent want to become leaders in their organizations |
| Tech Connected | 90 percent use the internet; 66 percent own a smartphone; 87 percent involved in social networking |
| Education | 54 percent have at least some college, compared to 36 percent of baby boomers |
| Social Responsibility | 86 percent want to work for employers who are socially responsible |
| Achievement Driven | 88 percent have established specific goals for the next five years |
| Multi-tasker | 55 percent believe multi-tasking yields helpful results |

**Envisioning the future**

In anticipation of these future trends and workforce characteristics, as a leader enmeshed in the Three Essentials of Leadership—education, experience, and exposure—you are technically prepared to deal with the consequences. It would be important, however, to remain abreast of external matters that impact your organization and make the appropriate and necessary adjustments to mitigate them. One area that cannot be overlooked moving forward is the requirement to work in a political environment that will continue to be, putting it mildly, dynamic. Leaders must certainly remain attuned to its ebbs and flow, but more importantly, must ensure during these times that organizational vision, values, and strategies provide an environment where different political views are accepted, but do not undermine organizational values and practices.

At Cuyahoga, I can envision our responses expanding as needs become more diverse and complex. It will become necessary to identify and develop individuals who can lead in this environment. Succession planning programs, like the "Nine Block" process, permit organizations to identify individuals who have the potential to assume increasingly more responsibility. One mechanism at Cuyahoga for providing this development is the Jack, Joseph, and Morton Mandel Leadership Program—a holistic approach to professional development that provides elements of leadership training combined with mentoring, alternative work experience, and teamwork.

Despite the success of Mandel and other programs, I am convinced current leadership programs will need to be transformed; crafted for individuals and networks. In the following diagram, Nick Petrie, of the Center for Creative

Leadership, compared current leadership development against how it might be focused in the future.

| Current Focus | Future Focus |
|---|---|
| The "what" of leadership | The "what" and "how" of development |
| Horizontal development | Horizontal and vertical development |
| Human Resources and training companies own development | Each person owns his or her development |
| Leadership resides in individual managers | Collective leadership is spread throughout the network |

Petrie suggests that methods used in the past will not be sufficient for the complexity of challenges that will reflect organizations and broader society. He believes leadership development must be thought of as a shared process rather than an individual skill set. Further, leadership spread throughout a network of people is more likely to flourish when certain conditions support it. These include:

**More focus on vertical development.** Horizontal development can be transmitted from an expert. Vertical development, however, is a move away from isolated behavioral competencies and toward complex thinking abilities. These appear as adaptive competencies, such as learning agility, self-awareness, comfort with ambiguity, and strategic thinking—all of which result in leading creatively.

**Transfer of greater developmental ownership to the individual.** As with vertical development, people develop fastest when they feel responsible for their own progress. The current model encourages people to believe that someone else is responsible for their development—human resources, their manager, or even trainers.

**Greater focus on collective rather than individual leadership.** There is a transition occurring from the old paradigm, where leadership resided in a specific department, to a new one where leadership is a collective process spread throughout networks of people. The question will change from, "Who are the leaders?" to "What conditions do we need for leadership to flourish in the network?" and "How do we spread leadership capacity throughout the organization and democratize leadership?"

**Much greater focus on innovation in leadership development methods.** There are no simple existing models or programs sufficient to develop the levels of collective leadership required to meet an increasingly complex future. Instead, an era of rapid innovation is necessary, one in which organizations experiment with new approaches that combine diverse ideas in new ways and share these with others. Technology and the web will provide the infrastructure and drive the change. Organizations that embrace these changes will do better than those that resist it.

**The community college continuing imperative**
At the center of worker and leader development is aligning it with external and internal realities that will enable organizations to continue to thrive. Let's look at the community college sector as an example.

As portrayed in the 2012 report from the American Association of Community Colleges (AACC) *Reclaiming the American Dream*, the connection between education and American prosperity is direct and powerful. National leaders typically have understood that the more educated people are, the more likely they are to be employed in jobs that can sustain a family and contribute to the economic vitality and democratic life of the nation.

Community colleges have played a crucial role in seizing this opportunity. Remember, in the year 2009 President Barack Obama believed if these institutions could participate in adding 20 million post-secondary-educated workers to its labor force by 2025, income inequality would decline substantially, reversing the erosion of the middle class. By the end of his administration, President Obama was even proposing free tuition for students who attended two-year institutions.

Despite this vote of confidence, community colleges still need to be redesigned for new times. What we observe today are student success rates that are unacceptably low; employment preparation inadequately connected to job market needs; and disconnects in transitions between high schools, community colleges, and baccalaureate institutions.

In their article "Are Community Colleges Preparing the Future Workforce?" Norman Augustine and Marc Tucker summarized, based on the findings of their report for the National Council on Education and the Economy, that this predicament could become a tragedy for many American community college students, but an even greater tragedy for the United States.

They found average real wages for workers have been falling for 20 years and will continue to fall if this country cannot produce a superior workforce that demands competitive wages.

American workers will not get jobs if they cannot compete academically. They will not have the more sophisticated kinds of knowledge and skills needed for future jobs as automation and outsourcing of work to China and India can be accomplished more cheaply.

These are just some of the challenges community colleges must address if they are to contribute to restoring the American Dream. They must reimagine their purposes and practices to meet the demands of the future, optimizing results for individuals, communities, and the nation.

## Cuyahoga responds

*Reclaiming the American Dream* is viewed as a viable framework for the many innovations needed at community colleges and those at Cuyahoga already described in *Changing the Lapel Pin*. That said, the trends cited by Vilmeete and Sele are too important to ignore. The college must implement additional measures that will enable it to not only improve outcomes—including graduation rates and numbers—but to educate more individuals through innovative programs and services that can be provided individually or online.

To accomplish this, we must provide access to more people categorized as "nontraditional" because they will constitute, as shown in the following chart, more than 75 percent of enrollment in community colleges. Only 25 percent of our future population at community colleges will be high school graduates from both traditional high schools and those that provide career and technical training.

## Nontraditional Students are the New Majority

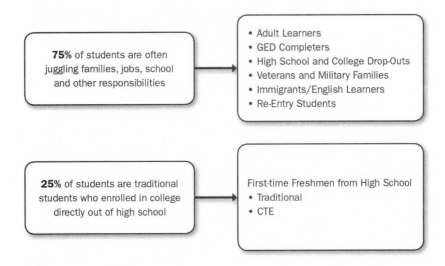

**75%** of students are often juggling families, jobs, school and other responsibilities

- Adult Learners
- GED Completers
- High School and College Drop-Outs
- Veterans and Military Families
- Immigrants/English Learners
- Re-Entry Students

**25%** of students are traditional students who enrolled in college directly out of high school

First-time Freshmen from High School
- Traditional
- CTE

Adult learners are among the nontraditional students who are already in the workforce and seek to improve their skills in preparation for a promotion or a job opportunity at another company. High school dropouts will seek to complete a GED in preparation for the workforce or to build a foundation for postsecondary education in pursuit of a certificate or a degree. For example, through the adult diploma program offered as part of Ohio's Aspire initiative, it is possible for individuals to simultaneously earn a high school diploma and a certificate. When the program was announced at Cuyahoga, one of three pilot sites in the state, 2,300 individuals applied for 350 funded slots. Given the enormous response, Cuyahoga funded an additional 150 individuals.

More veterans are expected to enter college as they better understand the benefits of the G.I. Bill, especially those who served following the tragedy of September 11, 2001. Cuyahoga has been deemed a "military friendly college," and has opened several centers for veterans—including one at the Louis Stokes Veterans Administration Hospital.

The number of incarcerated individuals re-entering society is also expected to grow. And we must increase specialized recruitment programs and consider building residential facilities—a growing interest at community colleges—to attract more national and international students. This may entail recruiting in expanding world markets in Asia, where residents will continue to depend on a respected American post-secondary education system to provide them with the education and training they need to secure jobs here and in their home countries.

Many of these non-traditional students will enter college through workforce and corporate training programs. Over the past several years, we have developed a significant number of short-term training programs ranging from a few weeks to one year in duration. Each lead to credentials that enable individuals to compete for emerging job opportunities that require generic and specialized skill sets. Cuyahoga increased the number of credentials awarded from 862 in 2013 to 13,903 in 2017.

As business trends continue to impact organizations, this provides an opportunity for Cuyahoga to train managers in its Corporate College on how to comply with government regulations, implement technology solutions, and become better leaders in response to this quickly evolving environment.

If the predictions come true, high school graduates

entering the college will level off. But before they complete their secondary education, some students will enroll in college courses concurrently with their high school classes. They will begin their post-secondary experiences early with a goal to earn a credential in welding or robotics or have an experience in cultural arts that personally enriches them.

The bottom line is that no matter what the future holds, internal barriers that limit access to the college must be eliminated. The student experience must be more rational, intentional, and even mandatory. Student-facing and behind-the-scenes staff must be given the knowledge and authority to make decisions that increase student satisfaction and success. For this purpose, technology such as Cuyahoga's One Record system will allow everyone to remain abreast of student interactions throughout the college.

New faculty are expected to be proficient in technology so they can advise students and teach more web-based courses and programs. And when appropriate, they must augment instruction with work-like experiences, including internships or service learning experiences that connect students with the communities served by the college.

Administrators must be attuned to and implement innovations—either on the fly or gradually—that increase productivity and complement the actions on the campuses that accentuate student access, equity, and success.

As you can see, the very nature of the world in the future will undoubtedly transform organizations and the individuals that will head them. Current and prospective leaders, therefore, must be equipped to be successful in this environment. This means identifying and developing prospective leaders through approaches that improve their on-the-job behavior, enrich the workplace, and provide training to enable them to perform at the highest levels possible. This process starts early when we assist workers exploit the training, experiences, and interactions that can serve as a foundation for their growth and possible ascension to a leadership role. We can no longer afford for this evolution to be unpredictable, given the leaders who have faltered because they have no reliable approach to leadership developed from within. *Change the Lapel Pin* helps you look inward.

# VIII. Lagniappe
*A little something extra.*

*C*hange *the Lapel Pin: Personalizing Leadership to Transform Organizations and Communities* represents a dramatic shift in how leadership is developed and applied. The approach is deeply rooted in my belief that good leaders can be developed organically from sources within that emanate from consequential life experiences, learning, and interactions with people. Natural talent is an intrinsic force in this approach which can be beneficial when identified, nurtured, and applied properly. And pertinent competencies and skills acquired during professional development— such as coaching—and through on the job encounters and maturation round out the personalized approach proposed in the book.

The leadership "idea" that somewhat approximates the Change the Lapel Pin model is "authentic leadership," where according to Dan McCarthy in "Authentic Leadership Development: Your Past, Present and Future," being a leader requires you to be sincere, genuine, and real. You lead from the heart and are true to your values and principles. Thus, you build trust, gain credibility, and inspire loyalty—all important characteristics of great leadership. McCarthy also believes that while studying leadership theories and styles increases knowledge, it does not substitute for identifying key moments that shaped your values, principles, and identity. And when you examine these incidents, you begin to piece together patterns that help define what's important to you today.

Like authentic leadership, the approach in *Change the Lapel Pin* concludes that your experiences are essential to becoming a good leader, but it also requires leaders to identify and hone natural gifts, to develop essential technical competencies and skills, and, as you evolve as a leader, to assimilate lessons learned around emotional intelligence. The impact of these elements can be observed and measured and the results of the assessments used to strengthen both the leader and the organization.

Why is the personalized approach captured in *Change the Lapel Pin* necessary at this time in history? In "The Dawn of System Leadership," Peter Senge, Hal Hamilton, and John Kania contend that "deep changes necessary to accelerate progress against society's most intractable problems require a unique type of leader ... a person who can catalyze collective leadership." This sentiment is evident across all ranks and levels as failed leadership is affecting not only businesses, but the common good when you consider the political climate and its erosion of Americans' trust in our public officials and systems.

According to Laci Lowe of the Brandon Hall Group, much of the dysfunction of leaders comes from three areas.

**Failure to build personal accountability.** Leaders allow the efforts of the organization they serve to advance personal goals. They fail to cultivate a circle of peers and solicit candid feedback about their decisions and maintain a personal system of checks and balances.

**Poor integrity/lack of trust.** Bad leaders guard their reputations so strongly, they aren't willing to own poor decisions, share truth, or pursue the most honorable path. They purposefully elect to conceal details, hide facts, misrepresent data, and make unsound decisions in a selfish attempt to protect their personal brand and/or achieve their personal goals and desires at the expense of others.

**Couldn't happen to me syndrome.** What is possibly most disturbing is leaders who do not learn from the failures of others and choose to continue similar behaviors that can lead to the same disastrous outcome. Regardless of competence, an arrogant leader will ultimately serve as the organization's point of failure—it is just a matter of when.

At the heart of this self-destruction are deficiencies that perhaps more emotional intelligence, experience, and training might counteract. However, more training may not be the answer according to Michael Beer, Magnus Finnström, and Derek Schrader in "Why Leadership Training Fails—and What to do About It." The authors found that American companies spend enormous amounts of money on employee training and education, but they are not getting a good return on their investment. For the most part, the learning doesn't lead to better organizational performance, because people soon revert to their old ways of doing things.

And finally, theories of leadership may be an issue. Doug Sundheim, in the "The Trouble with Leadership Theories," believes they are useful in pulling together disparate ideas and data into working models, distinguishing concepts, and for providing a systemic perspective. But the trouble with leadership theories is they are easy to hide behind, often inaccurately. They become proxies for actual leadership. "When something important is on the line, people don't follow five-tiered triangles, four-box matrices, or three concentric circles. They follow real people," proclaims Sundheim.

The three debilitating factors, the issues with training, and the possible lack of understanding of how to apply leadership theories, in combination, may result in some leaders not possessing a consistent and dependable approach or style. And, as a result, their leadership is ineffective, even compromised. The only bright side to revelations of such leadership failure is the opportunity for dramatic course correction, according to Lowe.

*Change the Lapel Pin*, I believe, provides this course correction for the reasons cited throughout the book. It is nurtured by your personal experiences and encounters—whether good or bad. It helps you identify, strengthen, and apply your natural talents. And it calls upon you to develop core competencies through training and while working. The skills you develop are applicable to a variety of settings. As a result, *Change the Lapel Pin* contains a most reliable and constant approach to leadership that serves you steadfastly, regardless of the circumstance. In other words, you become more authentic.

What does this leadership look like in actuality? It looks very much like the leaders described in this book who toiled at the community level, such as Rubie McCullough, Founder and President of the Lee Harvard Community Services Center, and those who served at the corporate level, including Howard Schultz, Chairman of Starbucks.

Like them, you become closer to the people who do the work, both personally and structurally. You seek and recognize engagement that leads to good outcomes. You rely on the foundations of the organization—vision, values, and strategies—to arrest challenge and controversy. You gain competence as a strategist and tactician. You learn ways of determining how culture can be used to strengthen and advance the organization. You develop on the job, achieving heightened competence in relational leadership where you thrive on persuasion and consensus, as opposed to using your position as the base of power. You create a narrative around values and behaviors that will serve the organization beyond your tenure. At its core, the personalized leadership advocated in *Change the Lapel Pin* allows you and the organization to transform communities and lives. And this is important now more than ever.

As a leader, think about the usefulness of this approach, not only for yourself, but for the future generations who will follow in your path. After all, exposure is one of the Three Essential Elements. This interaction can take the form of a succession planning program. But one-on-one interactions sometimes are preferable to a formalized approach. It is about the future. We do not like to talk about our "legacy." We are humble. And the idea of a legacy, in our minds, smacks of pretentiousness. Despite this concern, you *will* leave behind a legacy of sorts. Start now by deciding to make your legacy meaningful and allow *Change the Lapel Pin: Personalizing Leadership for Organizations and Communities* to serve as your guide for this action.

One other thing, take charge of your physical and emotional well-being, a reminder recently from my friend Beth E. Mooney, Chairman and CEO of KeyCorp. A sound mind and body and healthy relationships with family, friends, and colleagues contributes to the clarity required to carry out your professional obligations. I am by no means the expert on this subject. In recounting my leadership journey, many professional successes and challenges come to mind. Even more memorable now are the unintended consequences. I did not recognize them fully during my leadership journey, but they cause me to lament toward its end. During family gatherings, my children reminisce about important events and activities I do not recall because I was not there.

Do not let this happen to you. Enjoy the journey, but honor the balance between work and life-sustaining relationships.

# Acknowledgements

This book began in January 2009 as a way to honor the life of a good friend, Robert Calloway. He was a family man, a man of God, and a staunch advocate of the two-year college as a change agent for lives and neighborhoods. In the midst of celebrating Robert, it became clear to me that his life of learning, leading, and serving could help organizations and communities beyond Lorain County, Ohio where he lived and worked. It was Robert's example that inspired me to think about a form of leadership that emerges from one's personal life; that when combined with specific skills and competencies and on-the-job learning will serve them steadfastly throughout the leadership journey.

I want to thank the editorial team from Smart Business Books, especially Dustin S. Klein and Dennis Seeds, who encouraged me to finish *Change the Lapel Pin* after a long hiatus. They believed I had a story to tell that would help individuals to look within for core values and experiences on which to base their leadership approaches.

My associates at the community colleges where I served have provided some of the impetus for *Change the Lapel Pin* through their demonstrated passion for students. In this vein, and while overcoming the ravages of Hurricane Katrina, I benefitted from the unswerving loyalty of my Delgado Community College colleagues: Debbie Lea, Arnel Cosey, Carmen Walters, Thomas Lovince, Steve Cazaubon, Adolfo Girau, Kathleen Mix, and Larissa Littleton-Steib, who is continuing her leadership journey as chancellor at Baton Rouge Community College in Louisiana.

From the Community College of Allegheny County, I wish to acknowledge Mary Frances Archey, Joyce Breckenridge,

Bonita Richardson, Ouida Duncan, John Dziak, and Patty Zahurak for their unswerving dedication to students in the face of financial hardship and political challenge. And deep appreciation to my Allegheny colleagues David Hoovler, Alicia Booker, and Donna Imhoff who have since joined me at Cuyahoga Community College.

I am deeply indebted to my colleagues among the faculty and staff at Cuyahoga Community College for their support, especially to those who made the commitment to student completion and success a top priority. Mary Hovanec and Ed Foley, along with all members of the President's Cabinet, the President's Council, the College-wide Cabinet, Student Success Teams, and other groups and individuals have been at the forefront of this effort. Those who participated in the "One Door, Many Options for Success" deliberations created a research and development think tank that will serve the college throughout the years. And I am fortunate to have in my office some of the finest and most loyal and hardworking people I know: Ronna McNair, Stacey Brubeck, Barbara Bell, Gloria Moosmann, Kay Williams-Jones, and Jenneffer Lopez. Thanks to Eric Wheeler for creating the charts and diagrams for the book.

As I consider my leadership journey, I have benefitted from the support of individuals beyond the walls of academia. In this category are longtime friends (and in a few cases, golf buddies), not described in the book, but who have been sources of fun, inspiration, and support. Among them are John Brown, Clayton Harris, The Honorable Frank Jackson (Mayor of Cleveland), Jerry Lopes, Carole Hoover, Edgar Jackson, Randell McShepherd, Darrell McNair, Andrea Hogben, Valarie McCall, and Alden Macdonald.

A special acknowledgment to my mentee, Aujah

Thompson, who I met during her sixth-grade year and who is now completing her second year at prestigious Allegheny College. I am proud of her.

My family's love has been unconditional throughout this process. They have been my staunchest supporters, even when my writing detracted from their time with me. My daughter, Dr. Kim Johnson, evaluated my writing more thoroughly than I critiqued her work during her schooldays. My son Nakia, a tremendously talented writer, and his wife Shamuire have been cheerleaders for this venture. And hopefully my grandbabies, Ruby and Rory, will understand the book's reason and relevance in the future. My siblings, Derek Davis, Janet Mitchell, Pamela Benjamin, and Angela Green, along with my "auntie" Marva Cook and uncle Dennis Johnson, have been sources of encouragement throughout the years, as have been John, Doshia, Joy, and Jason Banks

Nothing was more constant in my life over the last 45 years than the loving support of my wife, Daphne. For this, I am truly grateful.

# Notes

## I. Introduction

Kevin Kelloway, Niro Sivanathan, Lori Francis, and Julian Barling, "Poor Leadership," in *Handbook of Work Stress* by Julian Darling, Kevin Kelloway and Michael Frone. (Thousand Oaks: Sage Publishing Incorporated, 2004).

Thomas Mann and Norman Ornstein. "Finding the Common Good in an Era of Dysfunctional Government." *Daedalus*, Spring, 2013.

## II. The Remnants and Rudiments of My Personalized Approach to Leadership

Barbara Brown Taylor. *Leaving Church: A Memoir of Faith.* (San Francisco: HarperOne, 2012).

Frank Capra. *It's A Wonderful Life.* RKO Radio Pictures, December 20, 1946.

Cornel West. *Race Matters.* (Boston: Beacon Press, 1993).

George Ambler. "How Experiences Shape and Make Leaders." http://www.georgeambler.com/how-experiences-shape-and-make-leaders/

Leonard Schaeffer. "The Leadership Journey." *Harvard Business Review,* October 2002.

### III. Connecting the Fundamentals of the Personalized Approach

### IV. Charting the Three Essentials of Leadership

Phil Hinson and Anthony Sturgess. *Uncommon Leadership: How to Build Competitive Advantage by Thinking Differently.* (Philadelphia: Kogan Page, 2014).

Louis Stokes. *The Gentleman from Ohio.* (Columbus, OH: Trilium, 2016).

### V. Understanding and Applying the Origins of Leadership

Hillary Clinton for America. https://www.hillaryclinton.comhillary

Andrew King, Dominic Johnson, and Mark Van Vugt. "The Origins and Evolution of Leadership." *Current Biology,* October 2009.

Heather Fork. "What are Your Natural Gifts? Is Your Job Making the Most of Them?" *Doctors Crossing,* January 21, 2012.

Travis Bradberry. "5 Boneheaded Ways Smart People Fail." *Forbes,* September 27, 2016.

Paul Hersey. *The Situational Leader.* (New York: Warner Books, 1985).

Kenneth H. Blanchard. *The One Minute Manager*. (New York: William Morrow and Company, 1980).

Jim Collins. *Good to Great: Why Some Companies Make the Leap, and Others Don't*. (New York: HarperCollins, 2001).

E.D. Hirsch. *Cultural Literacy: What Every American Needs to Know*. (New York: Vintage, 1988).

Erika Andersen. "Are Leaders Born or Made?" *Forbes*, November 12, 2012.

## VI. <u>Competencies and Skills</u>

Michael Wilkins. *The First 90 Days: Critical Success Strategies for New Leaders at All Levels*. (Cambridge, MA: Harvard Business Review Press, 2013).

Glenn Llopis. "5 Ways Great Leaders Cultivate Wisdom in The Workplace." *Forbes,* May 25, 2014.

Alex Johnson. "Personal Pathways to the Presidency." *The Presidency Magazine*, Spring, 2009.

John Mayer and Peter Salovey. "The Intelligence of Emotional Intelligence." *Intelligence*, October- December 1993.

Sara Fletcher. "5 Reasons Why Emotional Intelligence is Critical in Leadership." *Lead Change Group*, May 4, 2017.

Daniel Goleman. "What Makes a Leader?" In *Harvard*

*Business Review on the Mind of the Leader*. (Cambridge, MA: Harvard Business School Publishing Corporation, 2005).

Mindtools. "Emotional Intelligence in Leadership." https://www.mindtools.com/pages/article/newLDR_45.htm

Patrick Lencioni. *The Advantage: Why Organizational Health Trumps Everything Else in Business*. (San Francisco, CA: Jossey-Bass, 2012)

Diane Contu. "Putting Leaders on the Couch: A Conversation with Manfred F.R. Kets de Vries." In *Harvard Business Review on the Mind of the Leader*. (Cambridge, MA: Harvard Business School Publishing Corporation, 2005).

Mark Coles. "Jeff Bezos." *BBC News.com profile*. http://www.bbc.co.uk/programmes/b01rqbhl

Sara Stibitz. "How to Really Listen to Your Employees." *Harvard Business Review*, January 30, 2015.

Carol Kinsey Gorman. "8 tips for Collaborative Leadership." *Forbes*, February 13, 2014.

Herminia Ibarra and Morton Hansen. "Are You a Collaborative Leader?" *Harvard Business Review*, July-August 2011.

Complete College America. *Time is the Enemy*. (Indianapolis, IN: Complete College America, 2011).

John Kotter. *Leading Change: Why Transformation Efforts*

*Fail.* (Cambridge, MA: Harvard University Press, 1996).

Patricia Dwyer. "Transforming a Core Curriculum and Minimizing the Battle Scars." *Liberal Education,* Winter, 2017.

Kamran Akbarzadeh. *Leadership Soup: A Healthy Yet Tasty Recipe for Living and Leading on Purpose.* (Bloomington, MN: Xlibris Corporation, 2011).

Toby Cosgrove. *The Cleveland Clinic Way: Lessons in Excellence from One of the World's Leading Health Care Organizations.* (New York: McGraw-Hill Education, 2014).

James Heskett. *The Culture Cycle: How to Shape the Unseen Force that Transforms Performance.* (Indianapolis, IN: Pearson FT Press, 2015).

Edgar Schein. *Organizational Culture and Leadership.* 5th *Edition.* (Hoboken, NJ: Wiley, 2016).

Bonnie Warren. "50 Years of Faith and Vision." *Biz the Magazine,* December 2014.

### VII.  Other Considerations

Jacob Morgan. "The Evolution of the Manager." *Forbes,* December 4, 2014.

Graham Jones. "Avoiding the Perils of the Accidental Leader." *Management Issues,* July 25, 2014.

National Commission on Excellence in Education. *A Nation At-Risk: The Imperative for Educational Reform.* (Washington, DC: United State Department of Education, 1983).

Kevin Berchelmann. "What Does Leadership Feel Like?" *Triangle Performance, LLC,* June 6, 2013.

Fawn Johnson. "How a Community College's Big Ideas are Transforming Education." *The Next America,* October 12, 2012.

American Association of Community Colleges. *Reclaiming the American Dream Community Colleges and the Nation's Future.* (Washington, DC: AACC, 2012).

Douglas Martin. "University of North Carolina President Dies at 92." *The New York Times,* October 12, 2012.

Jacqueline Smith. "What Inspires the World's Top Leaders." *Forbes,* July 24, 2013.

Lynn Offermann. "When Followers Become Toxic." In *Harvard Business Review on the Mind of the Leader.* (Cambridge, MA: Harvard Business School Publishing Corporation, 2005).

David Thomas and Robin Ely. "Making Differences Matter: A New Paradigm for Managing Diversity." *Harvard Business Review,* September 1996.

Josh Greenberg. "Diversity in the Workplace: Benefits, Challenges, and Solutions." http://www.

multiculturaladvantage.com/recruit/diversity/
diversity-in-the-workplace-benefits-challenges-
solutions.asp

DiversityInc. "The 2017 DiversityInc Top 50
Companies for Diversity." http://www.diversityinc.
com/the-diversityinc-top-50-companies-for-
diversity-2017/

Sara O'Brien and Laurie Segall. "Money, Power &
Sexual Harassment." *CNN Tech*, July 20, 2017.

Elizabeth Weise and John Swartz. "Diversity Debate
Divides Silicon Valley." *USA Today*. August 6, 2017.

Deloitte and the Alliance for Board Diversity. "A
Missing Pieces Report: The 2016 Board Diversity
Census of Women and Minorities on Fortune 500
Boards." https://www2.deloitte.com/content/dam/
Deloitte/us/Documents/center-for-corporate-
governance/us-board-diversity-census-missing-pieces.
pdf

Weber Shandwick and KRC Research. "The Dawn of
CEO Activism." http://www.webershandwick.com/
uploads/news/files/the-dawn-of-ceo-activism.pdf

Allison Gordon. "Cross-Generational Transfer of
Knowledge." https://www.slideshare.net/mobile/
allisong234/crossgenerational-knowledge-transfer

American Council on Education. *A Matter of
Excellence. A Guide to Strategic Diversity Leadership*

*and Accountability in Higher Education.* (Washington, DC: American Council on Education, 2013)

Jeremy Hyman and Lynn Jacobs. "Why Does Diversity Matter at College Anyway?" *US News Higher Education,* August 12, 2009.

Shana Lebowitz. "From Projects to a $2.3 Billion Fortune: The Inspiring Rags-to-Riches Story of Starbuck's Howard Schultz." *Business Insider*, May 30, 2015.

Andrew Sorkin. "Howard Schultz to Step Down as Starbucks Chief Next Year." *New York Times,* December 1, 2016.

George Vielmeete and Yvonne Sele. *Leadership 2030. The Six Megatrends You Need to Understand to Lead Your Company into the Future.* (New York: Amacom, 2014)

Pete Cappelli and Ann Travis. "The Performance Management Revolution. *Harvard Business Review,* October 2016.

Jacob Morgan. *The Future of Work: Attract New Talent, Build Better Leaders, and Create a Competitive Organization.* (Hoboken, NJ: Wiley, 2014).

J. Walker Smith and Ann Cluma. *Rocking the Ages: The Yankelovich Report on Generational Marketing.* (New York: Harper,1998).

Switch and Shift. "The Rise of Millennials in Leadership Roles." *Digitalist Magazine*, September 16, 2016.

Norman Augustine and Marc Tucker. "Are Community Colleges Preparing the Future Workforce." *The Hechinger Report*, May 30, 2013.

## VIII.     <u>Lagniappe</u>

Dan McCarthy. "Authentic Leadership Development. Your Past, Present, and Future." *Great Leadership*, June 11, 2012.

Peter Senge, Hal Hamilton, and John Kania. "The Dawn of System Leadership." *Stanford Social Innovation Review*, Winter, 2015.

Laci Lowe. "Leadership Gone Wild: 3 Traits of Failed Leaders." *Brandon Hall Group*, October 13, 2014.

Michael Beer, Magnus Finnstrom, and Derek Schrader. "Why Leadership Training Fails and What to Do About it." *Harvard Business Review*, October 2016.

Doug Sundheim. "The Trouble with Leadership Theories." *Harvard Business Review*, May 5, 2014.